Atelier BNK 2014-2022

## 目次
Contents

## イントロダクション
Introduction

アトリエブンクの主な活動の場である北海道は、大部分が亜寒帯地域に属しており冬季間は雪が多く寒さが厳しいことが何よりも大きな特徴である。一方、世界の亜寒帯地域の中でも低緯度に位置していることから、比較的自然光に恵まれ四季の変化が感じられる場所でもある。このことから雪や寒さに対する堅牢性と、注意深く外に開く開放性、この相反する二つの性格を併せ持つ建築手法を長年積み重ねてきた。この考えは現在でも多くのプロジェクトで受け継がれている。

本作品集は2014年から2022年の9年間に完成した建築18作品を集めたものであり、『Atelier BNK 2000-2014』（建築画報社）の続編にあたる。近年、地方では一層の人口減少が進み、衰退する風景がつくられてきた。この状況に対して簡単に解決策は見いだせないが、少なくともかつての賑わいを取り戻すのではなく、現状を見据えて縮小社会にふさわしいまちのあり方を模索すべきであろう。ここ数年、我々は具体的な建築づくりを通してまちの再編に寄与することを意識してきた。本作品集はその取り組みの記録でもある。

As the main area for Atelier BNK's undertakings, Hokkaido has most of its area in the subarctic region, and is primarily characterized by plenty of snow and severe cold during winter. On the other hand, since it is located at a lower latitude than other subarctic regions around the world, Hokkaido is also a place that is relatively blessed with natural light where one can experience the seasonal changes. Because of this, we have built up construction techniques over the years to combine two contradictory features—robustness against snow and cold as well as openness for guardedly opening up to the outdoors. That concept continues to live on today in many of our projects.

This collection gathers together 18 architectural works completed in the nine years between 2014 and 2022, and is a sequel to "Atelier BNK 2000–2014" (Kenchiku Gahou Inc.). Populations in regional areas continue to fall in recent years, creating a landscape of decline. Although finding solutions to this situation is not easy, we should at least look at actual conditions and explore community approaches that are appropriate for a shrinking society, instead of trying to recover the flourishing communities of the past. Over the last few years, we have intentionally worked to help restructure communities through specific building architectures. This collection of works also serves as a record of these efforts.

# 合理性から生態学的必然性へ

山田 深

## 公共と複合のプログラム

　地方都市の公共建築においては、様々な機能を複合化し一体として計画することが一般化しつつある。これは施設を単に効率的に計画することを意図するのみならず、複合化によって生まれる"相乗効果"のようなものを期待してもいるだろう。近年のアトリエブンクの作品群を一望してみると、このような地方都市の中核を担うであろう公共的な複合建築が特に重要な位置を占めているように思われる。また学校建築においても、小中あるいは中高のような複合化が行われている。公共施設の複合化自体は全国的な流れではあるが、アトリエブンクはこの現代的課題に対して、北海道という気候風土を前提としながら、建築的かつ空間的に真摯に取り組もうとしているように見える。それは単にプログラムを解くという以上に、公共性/複合性/積雪寒冷地という問題群の中に、新たな北海道の建築を構築する可能性を見出しているのだと思われる。現在の設計全体を統括する加藤誠を軸として、ここにアトリエブンクの骨太な方向性が明確に現れてきている。

## 黒松内中学校・糸魚小学校からの展開

　これまで数々の興味深い作品を創りだしてきている中でも、ターニングポイントとして特に重要なものの一つが「黒松内中学校エコ改修」(2007)だろう。ここでは、光・温熱環境・構造・計画という相互に異なる領域を、横断的に統合して解を導く新たな方法論をつくり出した。従来より、ア

トリエブンクにはエンジニアリングを表現の根底に置いて思考する傾向があるといえるが、黒松内中学校においても、エンジニアリングをベースとした合理性の観点から、その原理的な方法論をスマートに構築してみせたといえる。これはその後の展開へとつながる建築の"モデル(型)"のようなものだと捉えることができ、おそらく加藤自身もそのことを明確に自覚しているものと思われる。

　一方、「糸魚小学校」(2008)は小学校に求められる多様なアクティビティへの対応が根底にあったと思われるが、黒松内中学校の原理的な在り方と比較すると、より自由で多彩な空間へと展開しているように見える。それはラクダの瘤のように上部に突き出した二つの大きな空間が互いに異なる方向を向いており、さらにその下部のルーバー状の梁の存在によって、単純には割り切れない豊かな彩りを空間内部につくり出していることなどにも現れている。

　このように黒松内中学校を合理的な建築の"モデル(型)"としながら、それを各種異なる条件において、公共性/複合性/積雪寒冷地へのより豊かな解法へと展開する近年の道筋が明確になったといえる。

## コンパクト化とワンルーム/複合化と関係性

　公共性/複合性/積雪寒冷地というプログラム上の課題を、具体的に統合して解くために見いだした建築的手法が、建築全体の"コンパクト化"であり、空間を"ワンルーム"のように扱うことであろう。そしてそこに異なる領域やプログラムを"複合化"することで、相互の"関係性"を創り出すことが強く意識されているように見える。積雪寒冷地における合理的な解釈としての建築形態の"コンパクト化"は、同時に施設計画における効率化も担保する。またコンパクト化されワンルーム的な空間においてプログラムを複合化することは、相互の"相乗効果"を高めるのに理にかなっている。そしてここで重要なのは、光や空気の流れという温熱環境を制御すると同時に建築全体に生気を与えるような空間が、すべてを複合化し関係づけるパラメーターとして位置づけられていること

である。このように見てくると、幾多の問題群を相互に関係づけることで、そこにポジティブに新たな北海道の建築のあり方を、方法論として構築しようとしているように思われる。

## 合理性と生態学的必然性

　このような展開の中で興味深いのは、作品に見られる"合理性"の様相が少し変化しつつあるように思われることである。それはかつてのエンジニアリング的な合理性というよりも、ある種の生態学的な必然性とでも呼ぶようなものへの変化である。

　例えば、「芽室町役場」(2021)の断面に現れる、議場の両側にうねるように立ち上がる2階への空気と光の通り道。また、「ニセコ町役場」(2021)の1階を覆う屋根スラブのめくり上がるような断面形状。あるいは「鷹栖地区住民センター」(2019)の屋根面の3つの異なる開口形状。さらには「名寄南小学校」(2016)の内部に挿入された二つの大胆なヴォイド空間。これらは、比喩的に例えて言えば、森の中で光を求めて上へ上へと伸びて生きようとする植物などの生態的なあり方とも近いように思われてくる。糸魚小学校の二つのラクダの瘤も同様であろうが、ドライな合理性という以上に、建築全体に生き生きとした血流を促すような重要な空間となっているように見える。

　このことは、加藤が近年、温熱環境的な「ムラ」を意図的につくり出す可能性について研究を進めていることとも無関係でないように思われる。元来、北海道においては、温熱環境的なムラをつくることはタブーとされ、内部空間は均質であるほど良いとされてきた。しかしエンジニアリングをベースとしながらも、より本質的な快適性や人間的な多様性へと北海道の建築を開く可能性を探るところへと踏み込みつつある。

　以上のようなアトリエブンクの近年の試みは、"北海道の建築"の新たなあり方を、具体的な方法論として我々に示してくれている。このような深い水準での"北海道の建築"の試みはかつてなかったであろうし、また北海道という枠組みを超えて、現代建築の方法論としても極めて意義深い試みであると思われる。

# From Rationality to Ecological Necessity

Shin YAMADA

## Public and complex programs

For public buildings in regional cities, it is becoming more common to combine their various functions and design them as one. This is done not merely with the intention to efficiently design the facilities, but also with the expectation that some kind of synergy will be created by this combination. Looking at the various works by Atelier BNK in recent years, such as building complexes for the general public, which play a central role in regional cities, appear to occupy a particularly significant position. Moreover, school buildings are also being combined, such as elementary and junior high schools, or junior high and high schools. While the move toward complexes for public facilities itself is a nationwide trend, Atelier BNK appears to be seriously tackling this contemporary issue architecturally and spatially, while taking the climate and geographical features of Hokkaido as a prerequisite. Rather than simply working on the program, Atelier BNK seems to be looking for the possibilities of building new architecture for Hokkaido even with the set of issues involving their public nature, their complexity, and the cold, snowy region. With Makoto Kato at the helm, overseeing current designs, the bold direction taken by Atelier BNK clearly appears here.

## Developments from Kuromatsunai Junior High School and Itoi Elementary School

Among the large number of deeply interesting works that they have so far conceived, one of the key turning points is probably the Kuromatsunai Junior High School Renova-

tion (2007). In this project, Atelier BNK created a novel methodology that spans across the different fields of lighting, thermal environment, structure, and planning, and integrates them to arrive at a solution. Over the years, Atelier BNK has shown a tendency to approach works with engineering at the foundation of its expression. At Kuromatsunai Junior High School, we can see this principled methodology demonstrated through its smart construction from the perspective of rationality based on engineering. This may be considered as a kind of architectural model that has led to other developments thereafter, which Kato himself is probably quite conscious of.

On the other hand, Itoi Elementary School (2008) seems to have been based on responding to the variety of activities required of elementary schools, and compared to the principled approach in Kuromatsunai Junior High School, it seems to have developed into a freer and more diverse space. This is also reflected by the fact that two large spaces project from the top like camel's humps facing each other in different directions, as well as by the presence of louver-like beams at their base, creating a multitude of rich colors in the interior space.

Hence, while Kuromatsunai Junior High School is a model of rational architecture, the path in recent years toward developing this into richer solutions under varying conditions for the public nature, complexity, and the cold, snowy region has become more evident.

## Compactification and open plan spaces / Their complexity and relationships

The architectural approach that was found to concretely and comprehensively solve programmatic issues on the public nature, complexity, and the cold, snowy region is the compactification and open plan spaces. And by combining different fields and programs, there seems to be a strong intent to create mutual relationships. Compactification as the rational interpretation in the cold, snowy regions also ensures efficiency in facility planning. Additionally, combining programs in a compactified open plan spaces makes sense in enhancing their mutual synergy. The key here is in defining the space—controlling the thermal environment, such as the flow of light and air, and simultaneously giving vitality to the entire building—as a parameter that combines and interrelates everything. From this perspective, by interrelating the many sets of issues with each other, it seems that Atelier BNK is attempting to positively construct a new vision of architecture in Hokkaido through methodology.

## Rationality and ecological necessity

The interesting thing about these developments is that the aspect of rationality found in the works seems to be slightly changing. This is a shift toward what might be called some kind of ecological necessity, in lieu of the engineering rationality of the past.

One example is the air and light passage undulating upward on both sides of the assembly hall toward the second floor, appearing in the cross section of Memuro Town Hall (2021). Another is the cross-sectional form of the roof slab encompassing the first floor of Niseko Town Hall (2021), which seems to curl up. Or, the three different shapes of apertures on the roof surface of Takasu District Residents Center (2019). Additionally, one other example is the two dynamic void spaces incorporated within Nayoro Minami Elementary School (2016). To use a metaphorical analogy, these may be linked to the ecological ways of plants and other life forms in forests which stretch upward in search of light, going ever higher in order to survive. Similarly, the two camel humps at Itoi Elementary School also seem to go beyond dry rationality to serve as essential spaces promoting the active flow of lifeblood throughout the entire building.

This is not entirely unrelated to Kato's recent research into the possibility of deliberately creating irregularities in the thermal environment. In Hokkaido, it was naturally taboo to create thermal irregularities, with the prevailing idea that the more uniform the interior space, the better. However, while remaining grounded in engineering, Atelier BNK is also gradually exploring the possibility of broadening Hokkaido's architecture toward more essential comfort and human diversity.

Their recent efforts described above have shown us a new vision of "Hokkaido architecture" through a concrete methodology. I believe that such deep attempts toward "Hokkaido architecture" have never been done before, and are also quite significant in going beyond the framework of Hokkaido as a methodology for contemporary architecture.

山田 深（やまだ しん）
建築家／室蘭工業大学准教授

Shin YAMADA
Architect, Associate Professor at Muroran Institute of Technology

1962年東京都生まれ。東京工業大学工学部建築学科卒業、同大学大学院修士課程修了。1990-97年武田光史建築デザイン事務所。室蘭工業大学助手、講師を経て、2014年より現職。専門は建築家の創作論・空間論。主な建築作品に「カトリック東室蘭教会聖堂」など。

Born in Tokyo in 1962. After graduating from the Department of Architecture and Building Engineering, School of Engineering, Tokyo Institute of Technology, he obtained his master's degree at the same university. He worked at Koji Takeda & Associates from 1990 to 1997. After working as a research assistant and lecturer at Muroran Institute of Technology, he assumed his current position in 2014. He specializes in creative theory and spatial theory for architects. His major architectural works include Catholic Higashi Muroran Church.

# 芽室町役場

Memuro Town Hall

—

2021

—

十勝地方に位置する芽室町の役場庁舎である。ま
ちの中心と公共施設群の結節点となる敷地を生か
し、歩いて回れるまちづくりの核となる開かれた
庁舎を目指した。

限られた敷地に正方形プランを重ねた表裏のない
デザインで、3階をセットバックさせて周囲の住宅
スケールに馴染む佇まいとした。四周に張り出し
た2階の深い軒下空間が雨や雪を防ぎ、まちと庁舎
の緩衝空間となって内外をつなぐ。全面ガラスで
囲われた1階は、街路と直結する3か所の出入口か
ら自由にアクセスすることができる。1階全体が町
民を受け入れる、ピロティを内部化したような空
間となることを意識した。

This project is for a town hall for Memuro Town, located
in the Tokachi region. Taking advantage of the site, which
serves as the focal point for the center of town and clusters of public facilities, we aimed to create an open town
hall at the core of a walkable town development.
With a straight design and a stacked square plan on
the limited site, the third floor was set back in order to
give it an appearance of blending with the scale of the
surrounding residential area. The deep space under the
eaves on the second floor, which overhang on all four
sides, protects against rain and snow, acts as a buffer
space between the town and the town hall, and con-
nects the inside to the outside. The first floor is entirely
enclosed in glass and can be freely accessed from
three entryways that are directly connected to the
streets. The space was designed to appear as if the pilotis were placed internally so that the entire first floor
can accommodate the townspeople.

東外観 / East facade

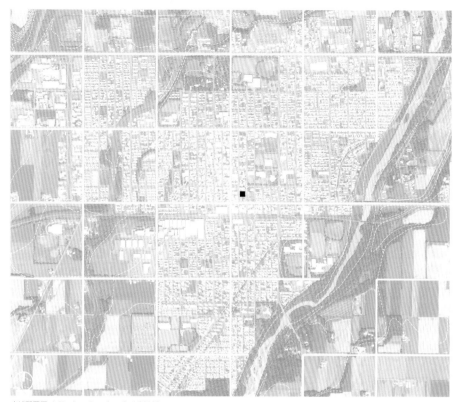

広域配置図 / Site location plan  S=1:30000

芽室の大地に広がる殖民区画を基軸としたグリッドパターン。
正方形プランを積層し、農業のまちを形象化する。

The grid pattern is based on the colonial demarcations across
the land in Memuro. The square plan is stacked to provide an
image of an agricultural town.

南鳥瞰 / Aerial view from the south

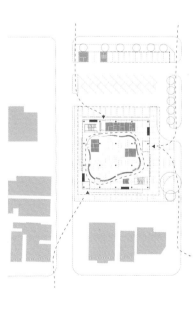

南東外観 / Southeast facade
外周4面に奥行きの違う庇を設け、歩行者を受け入れる。
Eaves of different depths are provided on the four sides of the building to accommodate pedestrians.

配置ダイアグラム / Layout diagram
街路と直結する3か所の出入口が内部ループ導線へとつながる。
Three entryways lead directly to the streets and connect to the interior pathway loop.

東外観 / East facade

1階全景 / Overall view of the first floor

1階執務室 / First floor office

正方形プランの中央に執務室を配置し、その周囲を回遊できる動線計画とした。執務室は課長席を設けないユニバーサルレイアウトを採用することで、無駄なスペースを省き効率化を図った。外周部が自然光や温度を吸収し、執務室の安定した温熱環境とムラのない光環境を獲得した。

構造は、広い執務空間を要する役場機能を考慮し、鉄骨ラーメン構造の1階に制震ダンパーを設ける制震構造を採用した。高い耐震性能を確保すると共に、将来の組織改編にも対応できるフレキシブルな庁舎を実現した。

The office space located at the center of the square plan while movement paths designed to go around it. The office area uses a universal layout without a chief desk, eliminating wasted space and boosting efficiency. The peripheral structure absorbs natural light and heat, providing even lighting and a stable thermal environment to the office area.

For the structure, considering that the building functions as a town hall which requires a large office space, a seismic control structure using seismic control dampers was installed at the first floor of the steel moment frame structure. Besides ensuring high seismic performance, this allowed for a flexible town hall that can accommodate future organizational changes.

Structure

構造ダイアグラム / Structural diagram

正方形プランを生かして1階四隅に耐力壁＋制震ダンパーをバランスよく配置。内部には耐力壁やブレースが不要となる計画。

Taking advantage of the square plan, load-bearing walls and seismic control dampers are evenly distributed at the four corners of the first floor. No load-bearing walls or braces are located in the interior.

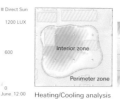

Daylight analysis　June_12:00　　Heating/Cooling analysis　Dec._12:00

インテリア・ペリメーターゾーンダイアグラム
Interior and perimeter zone diagram

カウンターで囲まれたインテリアゾーンに執務空間、ペリメーターゾーンに居場所・動線を配置した。一体空間でありながら執務空間を効率的に暖冷房し、日射の影響を受けないムラのない光環境、温熱環境を確保できる。

The office space is located in the interior zone and is enclosed by counters, while movement routes and sitting areas are laid out at the perimeter zone. While functioning as an integrated space, the office space is efficiently heated and cooled, ensuring a stable thermal environment with even lighting regardless of sunlight conditions.

1階待合スペース / First floor waiting area

3階平面図 / Third floor plan

2階平面図 / Second floor plan

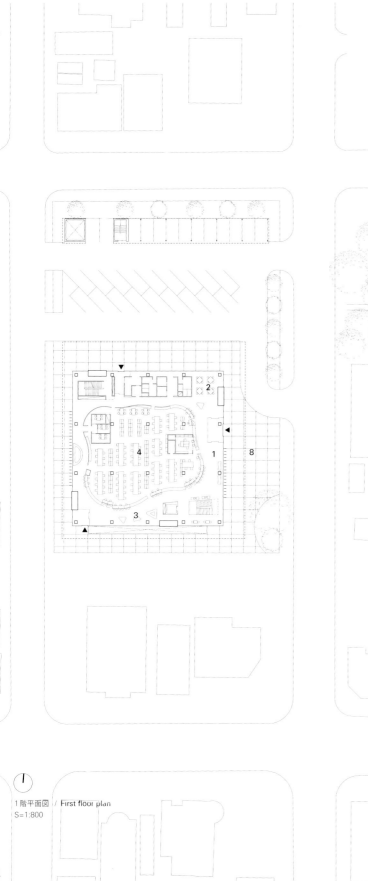

1階平面図 / First floor plan
S=1:800

地階平面図 / Basement floor plan

2階執務室吹抜 / Second floor office atrium

議場 / Assembly hall

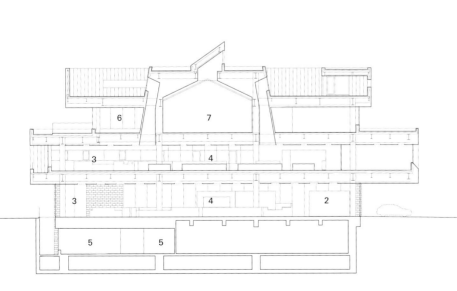

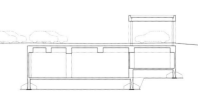

| 1. | エントランスホール<br>Entrance hall | 5. | 会議室<br>Conference room |
|----|----|----|----|
| 2. | 町民ホール<br>Community hall | 6. | 傍聴ラウンジ<br>Audience lounge |
| 3. | 待合スペース<br>Waiting area | 7. | 議場<br>Assembly hall |
| 4. | 執務室<br>Office | 8. | 町民広場<br>Town square |

断面図 / Cross-section view  S=1:400

# ニセコ町役場

Niseko Town Hall

——

2021

——

世界屈指のスキーリゾートであり先進的な環境への
取組で知られるニセコ町の新庁舎である。徒歩圏内
に公共施設や中心街が集約していることから、豪雪
や災害から町民生活を守ることを重視した。また、
環境配慮、町の魅力発信を同時に体現する庁舎を目
指した。市街地では珍しい3階建の新庁舎には、1
階屋根が大きく2、3階のヴォリュームを小さく抑
えた特徴的な断面を採用し、3階屋根からの落雪を
1階屋根で受け止め歩行者を守る構成とした。

This project is for the new town hall for Niseko Town, a
world-class ski resort known for progressive environ-
mental initiatives. Because the town center and public
facilities are clustered within walking distance, we fo-
cused on protecting the townspeople from heavy snow
and natural disasters. We also aimed for a town hall
that embodies both consideration for the environment
and promotion of the town's charms. The new three-story town hall—a rarity in an urban district—has a distinc-
tive cross section, employing a large roof on the first
floor while minimizing the volumes of the second and
third floors. We designed the structure to catch snowfall from the roof on to the first-floor roof to protect
pedestrians.

北西外観 / Northwest facade

西外観 / West facade

南西鳥瞰
Aerial view from the so

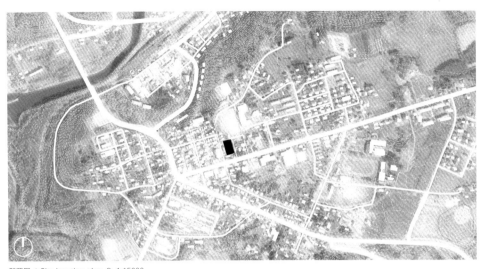

配置図 / Site location plan　S=1:15000
敷地は徒歩圏内に公共施設等が集約する中心市街地に位置する。羊蹄山とニセコアンヌプリを遠望できる。

The site is located in the town center, where public facilities and other buildings are clustered within walking distance. Mt. Yotei and Niseko Annupuri can be seen in the distance.

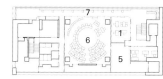

3階平面図 / Third floor plan

2階平面図 / Second floor plan

1. 執務室
   Office
2. 待合スペース
   Waiting area
3. 多目的ホール
   Multipurpose hall
4. 展示コーナー
   Display corner
5. 会議室
   Conference room
6. 町民ホール
   Town Hall
7. フリースペース
   Shared space
8. ポケットパーク
   Pocket park

2階待合スペース / Second floor waiting area

1階平面図 / First floor plan

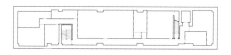

地階平面図 / Basement floor plan
S=1:1000

3階フリースペース / Third floor shared space

20

町民サービス窓口すべてを1階に集約し、町長室等の執務の中核を2階に配置。羊蹄山への大パノラマが広がる3階の町民ホールは円形の議場としても利用される。町の木であるシラカバを床・壁仕上げに採用し、共用部には町内家具作家によるオリジナル木製家具やアート作品を多数配置した。

All of the citizen service counters are concentrated on the first floor, while the core of official duties, including the mayor's office, is located on the second floor. The town hall on the third floor which offers a panoramic view of Mt. Yotei and is also used as a circular assembly hall. Japanese white birch—the town's symbolic tree—was used for the floors and wall finishings. Numerous original wooden furniture by a furniture designer in Niseko and artworks are arranged in the common area.

展示コーナーから1階執務室を見る / The first-floor office as seen from the display corner

議場としても利用される町民ホール
The town hall that is also used as the assembly hall

積雪風洞実験 / Snow and wind tunnel tests

CFD解析 / CFD analysis

模型を用いた積雪風洞実験とCFD解析から、積雪及び落雪の影響を
最小限とする形状を決定した。

We decided on a building form that minimizes the adverse
effects of snow cover and snowfall, based on snow and wind
tunnel tests using a scale model and CFD analysis.

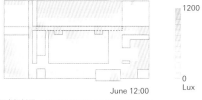

1200

0
Lux

June 12:00

1階床面照度解析図 / Floor lighting analysis diagram

階高の違いを生かし中央部にトップライトを設けた。熱負荷を考慮
し最小限の開口とし効果的に自然光を取り込む。

Skylights were installed at the central area to take advantage of
the difference in floor heights. Considering the heat load, the
openings are set to the minimum that effectively takes in natural
light.

1. 執務室
   Office

2. 待合スペース
   Waiting area

3. 書庫
   Stack space

4. 町民ホール
   Town Hall

5. フリースペース
   Shared space

執務室、トップライトからの光が落ちる待合スペース
The office, and the waiting area where light coming
from the skylight falls.

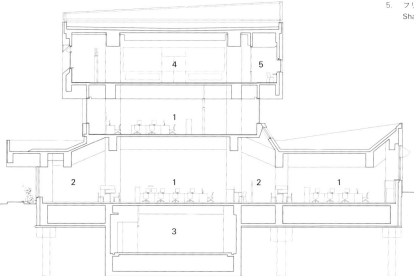

断面図 / Cross-section view  S=1:300

「SDGs 未来都市」に認定されたニセコ町は$CO_2$排出量の大幅削減目標を掲げており、本計画においては特に外皮性能を大幅に向上させた。外部サッシはすべて木製とし、アルゴンガス入りLow-Eトリプルガラスを採用した。壁・屋根面には高性能フェノールフォーム200mm相当の高い断熱性能を確保し、冷暖房負荷の徹底削減を図った。大自然の恵みと共に暮らし発展していく町・ニセコにおいて、新庁舎はその象徴としての役割を果たす。

Certified as an "SDGs Future City," Niseko Town has set a substantial carbon dioxide emissions reduction target. For this project, we paid close attention to significantly improving the performance of the outer shell. For the windows, low-E triple-pane glass filled with argon gas was used while the exterior sashes are all made of wood. High heat insulation performance equivalent to 200 mm of high-performance phenolic foam was ensured for the walls and roof surface to minimize heating and cooling loads. The new town hall serves as a symbol of Niseko, a town that lives and develops alongside the gifts of the great nature.

# 津別町役場

Tsubetsu Town Hall

—

2022

—

オホーツク圏内陸部に位置する愛林のまち・津別町における複合庁舎である。まちなか再生の中心施設として計画され、木のまちにふさわしい木材利用・地場産材への配慮・地元産業の振興が求められた。

主たる執務機能を開放的な木造空間とし、その周囲を堅牢なRCで取り囲む「入れ子型」の混構造を採用した。内部では木とコンクリートが素材のままに対峙し、重厚さの中に軽やかな木が飛び交う空間を目指した。

This project is for a government building complex in the tree-loving town of Tsubetsu, located inland of the Okhotsk area. The building was planned as a central facility to revitalize the central area of the town. The design required the use of timber befitting of the tree-centered town, consideration for locally produced wood, and promotion of local industries.

We opted for a nested mixed structure, in which the main office function uses an open wooden space while its surrounding area is enclosed by robust rein-forced concrete. Inside, we balanced the use of bare wood and concrete, with the aim of creating a playful-ly light wooden space amid a dignified atmosphere.

なみきロビー / Namiki Lobby

配置図 / Site location plan　S=1:25000

津別町の森林面積は、町の総面積の約8割以上を占める。古くから木材の加工・木製品の製造により林業に関連する産業が発展してきた。

The forested area of Tsubetsu Town occupies more than around 80% of its total land area. Industries related to forestry have developed here since the olden days, through wood processing and the manufacture of wooden products.

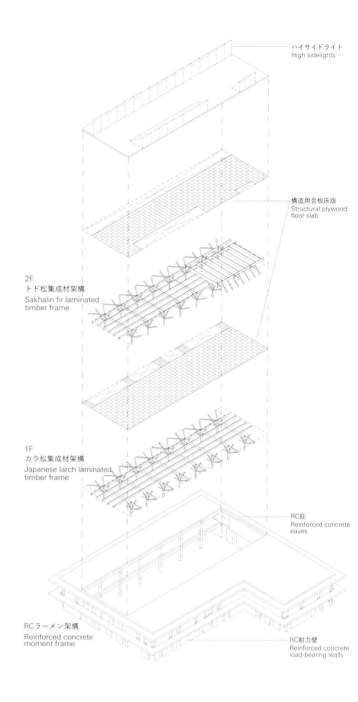

ハイサイドライト
High sidelights

構造用合板床版
Structural plywood floor slab

2F
トド松集成材架構
Sakhalin fir laminated timber frame

1F
カラ松集成材架構
Japanese larch laminated timber frame

RC庇
Reinforced concrete eaves

RCラーメン架構
Reinforced concrete moment frame

RC耐力壁
Reinforced concrete load-bearing walls

構造ダイアグラム / Structural diagram

外周部に配した厚さ400mmのRC耐力壁で建物全体の水平力を負担している。水平力から解放された木造部分は、180mm角方杖を四方に伸ばした樹形柱により梁成を抑えつつ、9.1mスパンを実現した。

The 400-mm thick reinforced concrete load-bearing walls positioned at the periphery bear the horizontal forces of the entire building. The wooden structure—free from bearing any horizontal forces—achieve 9.1-m spans while keeping beam depths small by using tree-like columns with 180-mm square diagonal braces extended in four directions.

建方時の状況 / During construction of the wooden structure

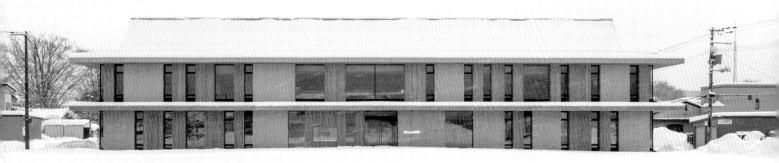

北外観 / North facade
正面キャノピー、外構工事が今後予定されている。
Front canopy and landscaping works are being planned.

西外観 / West facade

1階執務室 / First floor office

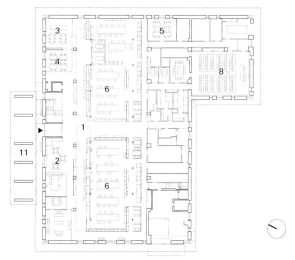

1階平面図 / First floor plan　S=1:800

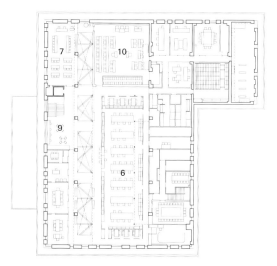

2階平面図 / Second floor plan

1. なみきロビー
   Namiki Lobby
2. 待合スペース
   Waiting area
3. 調理室
   Kitchen
4. ボランティア室
   Volunteer room
5. 活動室
   Activity room
6. 執務室
   Office
7. 会議室
   Conference room
8. 健診ホール
   Health screening hall
9. なみきラウンジ
   Namiki Lounge
10. 議場
    Assembly hall
11. キャノピー
    Canopy

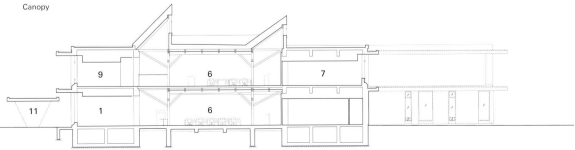

断面図 / Cross-section view　S=1:400

議場 / Assembly hall

構造材、内外装、家具造作、手摺、サインや職員のデスクに至るまで、あらゆる部位に町産木材を使用している。また、地場工場で生産される針葉樹構造用合板は、地場の加工技術により仕上げ材や家具などに活用し、素材としての様々な可能性を探った。外装は、町産カラマツ・トドマツの小角材を突き付けて合板に釘留めした簡素なつくりとし、地元職人の手で容易に張り替え可能な仕組みとしている。

地域の中で積み重ねられたものづくりの知見が、まちづくりにも展開し、津別らしい風景の創出につながることを期待している。

Locally produced timber was used throughout—for the structural materials, interior and exterior claddings, furniture and fixtures, handrails, signs, and staff desks. We explored the possibility of new building materials. Using local processing technology, structural plywood made from coniferous trees and produced at local factories were utilized as much as possible for finishings as well as furniture. The exterior cladding utilizes a simple construction, in which scantlings made from local Japanese larch and Sakhalin fir trees are held and nailed to plywood, for easy replacement by local craftsmen.

We hope that the craftsmanship knowledge that has been built up within the local community will also be applied to town development and ultimately lead to the creation of a unique Tsubetsu landscape.

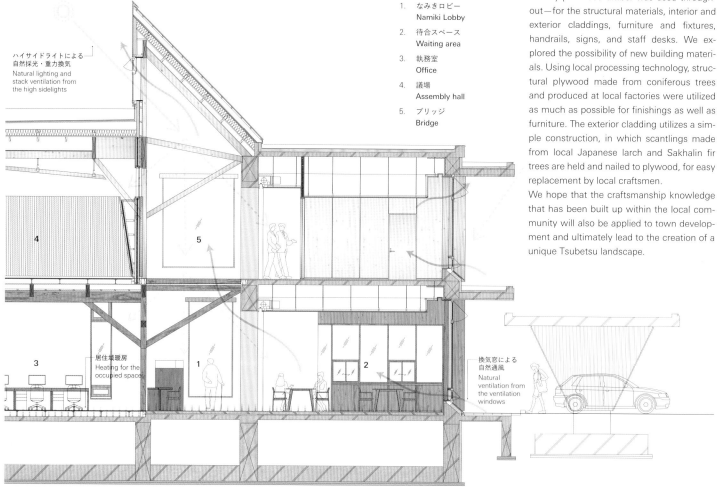

1. なみきロビー
   Namiki Lobby
2. 待合スペース
   Waiting area
3. 執務室
   Office
4. 議場
   Assembly hall
5. ブリッジ
   Bridge

ハイサイドライトによる自然採光・重力換気
Natural lighting and stack ventilation from the high sidelights

居住域暖房
Heating for the occupied space

換気窓による自然通風
Natural ventilation from the ventilation windows

矩計図 / Section detail drawing S=1:120
2層吹抜を活用した自然採光と重力換気により照明・空調コストを低減する。
Lighting and air conditioning costs are reduced by the use of natural lighting and stack ventilation utilizing a two-story atrium.

2階吹抜 / Second floor atrium

# 夕張市拠点複合施設 りすた

Yubari City Community Base Complex RESTA

—

2019

—

かつて石炭の町として栄えた夕張市は、急激な人口減少と高齢化の社会情勢に対応するため、公共施設を清水沢地区に集める「集約型コンパクトシティ」を将来像に掲げた。本施設はコンパクトシティの核となるもので、JR廃線後の代替交通となるバスのターミナル、図書・公民館機能、子育て支援・児童館機能、市役所支所を合わせてもつ市民のための「小さなまち」のような複合施設である。南に開き、北で絞る台形状平面とし、かつて神社があった鎮守の森への視線の抜けに配慮し、裏表なくバスターミナル利用者と森のつながりを生み出した。

Previously a prosperous coal-mining town, Yubari City adopted the concept of an "intensive compact city," with public facilities clustered in the Shimizusawa area, as its future vision of the city in order to adapt to the social conditions marked by the rapid decline and aging of the population. This facility is designated as the core of this compact city and is a complex facility similar to a "compact city" for the citizens, combining a bus terminal, to provide an alternative means of transportation after discontinuation of the JR Line, a library/public hall function, a childcare support/children's hall function, and a branch of the city hall. Its trapezoidal floor plan opens up to the south and narrows to the north, creating a direct link between bus terminal users and the forest in consideration of the loss of the line of sight to the forest where the local small shrine once stood.

南鳥瞰 / Aerial view from the south

35

コンパクトシティ化を図るため、官民の住宅群の建設及び道路インフラの整備が進む「りすた」を中心とする市街地。廃線となったJRに代わり、バスターミナル機能をもつ拠点施設が新しい「まちの駅」となり、人と車の結節点となる。

In order to create a compact city, construction of public and private housing complexes and road infrastructure will proceed. A base facility with bus terminal functions will replace the closed JR line as the new "town station" and serve as a node for people and cars.

JR廃線後の「りすた」を中心とする市街地。
Urban district revolving around RESTA after discontinuation of the JR Line.
S=1:25000

南外観 / South facade

南東外観 / Southeast facade

待合交流スペースから多目的ホールを見る。
The multipurpose hall as seen from the waiting and socializing area.

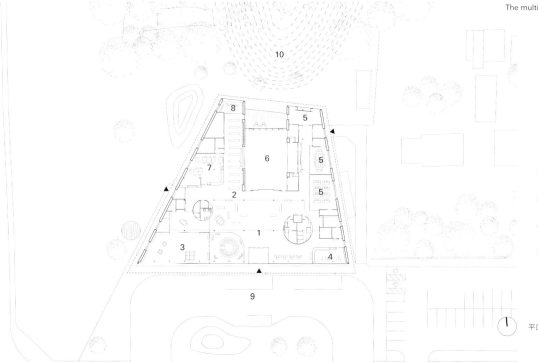

1. 待合交流スペース
   Waiting and socializing area

2. 図書コーナー
   Library corner

3. 児童・乳幼児スペース
   Children's and infants' area

4. 支所事務室
   Branch office

5. 多目的室
   Multipurpose room

6. 多目的ホール
   Multipurpose hall

7. 教育委員会
   Board of Education

8. 学習室
   Study room

9. バスロータリー
   Bus terminal

10. 鎮守の森
    Forest of the local small shrine

平面図 / Plan  S=1:1000

児童・乳幼児スペース / Children's and infants' area

深い庇を設けた南面ガラススクリーン、ルーバーで拡散する
ハイサイドライト、森の反射光を取り込む北面カーテンウォ
ールにより、年間を通じて奥行きの深い平面の中に光の濃淡
をつくる。

The south-facing glass screen with deep eaves, the high
sidelight that diffuse light using louvers, and the north-fac-
ing curtain wall that captures reflected light from the
forest create light and shade in the deep floor plan all
through the year.

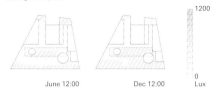

|       | 1200 |
|-------|------|
| June 12:00 | Dec 12:00 | 0 Lux |

床面照度解析図 / Floor lighting analysis diagram

構造は、耐力壁やブレースを外周部にのみ配
して8.1mグリッドで円柱を立てる軽快な鉄骨
平屋造を採用し、求められた機能を、入れ子
やガラススクリーンにより区切られた空間に
ゆるやかに配した。

We adopted a light steel single-story structure
with load-bearing walls and braces arranged only
at the perimeter, and round columns erected on
an 8.1-m grid. The required functions were loosely
distributed over the space separated by nesting
and glass screens.

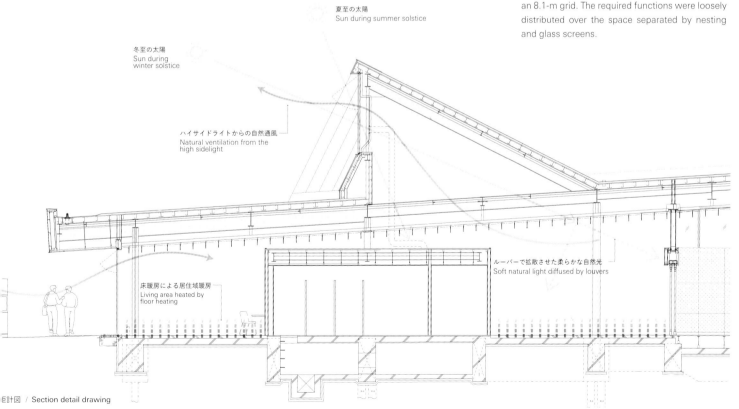

夏至の太陽
Sun during summer solstice

冬至の太陽
Sun during winter solstice

ハイサイドライトからの自然通風
Natural ventilation from the high sidelight

ルーバーで拡散させた柔らかな自然光
Soft natural light diffused by louvers

床暖房による居住域暖房
Living area heated by floor heating

断面詳細図 / Section detail drawing

待合交流スペース / Waiting and socializing area

1. 待合交流スペース
   Waiting and socializing area
2. 図書コーナー
   Library corner
3. 学習室
   Study room
4. バスロータリー
   Bus terminal
5. 鎮守の森
   Forest of the local small shrine

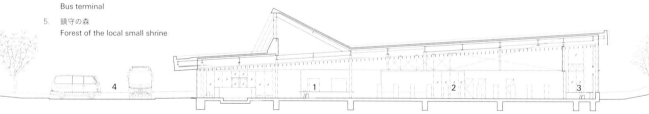

断面図 / Cross-section view　S=1:400

屋根を北側の森から南面に向かって傾斜を付けて、天井高の異なる空間をつくり、中央に大きな南面ハイサイドライトを設けた。天井高が抑えられた明るい南面は子どもが利用する部屋、高天井の静かな北面の空間には学習室等を配置した。大きな一枚屋根の下で異なる機能が一体感をもって広がる。

The roof slants downward from the forest at the north toward the south to create a space with varying ceiling heights, and has large, high sidelight installed at the center facing southward. A room for children's use is located on the bright south side where the ceiling height is low, and a study room and other rooms are located at the quiet north side space with a high ceiling. Different functions are spread out with a unified sense under one large roof.

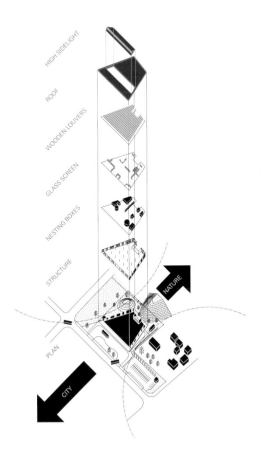

コンセプトダイアグラム / Conceptual diagram

図書コーナー / Library corner

# 鷹栖地区住民センター
## Takasu District Residents Center

—

2019

—

旭川市に隣接する鷹栖町は、二つの地区が小さな市街地を形成し、その周辺に三つの農村地区が点在する。市街地のひとつである鷹栖地区の住民センターの建て替えにあたり、公民館機能に図書館機能を複合し、多世代が交流できる新たなまちの拠点とすることが目論まれた。

建物はホールを中央に据えたコンパクトな平屋とし、周囲の住宅スケールに合わせることを意識した。勾配屋根が隣り合う住宅地に溶け込み、四周の深い庇は雪から来館者を守り迎え入れる。シンプルな矩計平面に大きな中庭をくり貫き、公民館機能と図書館機能が中庭を介して一体的につながる計画とした。自然光が回り込む中庭周囲は町民が自由に過ごす居場所となる。

In Takasu, a town adjacent to Asahikawa City, two districts form small urban areas while three rural districts are spread across the surrounding area. When rebuilding the Residents Center for the Takasu District, one of the urban areas, the plan was to combine a new library function with the public hall function to make a new town center for intergenerational interaction.

The building was designed to be compact and single-story with a central hall, as to match the scale of surrounding residences. The pitched roof blends with the adjacent residential area, and the deep eaves on four sides protect and welcome visitors from the snow. The design hollows out a large courtyard from the simple rectangular plan in order to integrally connect the public hall and library functions via the courtyard. Encompassed by natural light, the area around the courtyard is a place where the townspeople can freely spend their time.

北外観 / North facade

配置図 / Site location plan S=1:15000
農地に囲まれた鷹栖地区。
The Takasu District surrounded by farmlands.

1. ロビー
   Lobby
2. 図書室
   Library
3. ホワイエ
   Foyer
4. ホール
   Hall
5. 展示ギャラリー
   Display gallery
6. 事務室
   Office
7. 多目的活動室
   Multipurpose activity room
8. 調理室
   Kitchen
9. 会議室
   Conference room
10. 中庭
    Courtyard

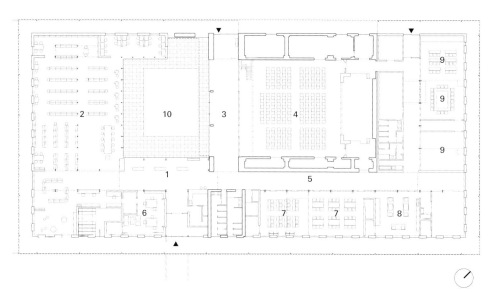

平面図 / Floor plan S=1:600

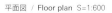

44

ロビー / Lobby

東外観 / East facade

積雪風洞実験 / Snow and wind tunnel test
冬の卓越風による吹き溜まりや雪庇の状況を検討し、中庭の積雪を抑えるように全体の形状を決定した。

We took into account of snowdrifts and overhanging snow caused by prevailing winds in winter, and decided on an overall configuration that can reduce snow accumulation in the courtyard.

展示ギャラリー / Display gallery

ホール / Hall

床面照度解析図 / Floor lighting analysis diagram
外周開口部、中庭、トップライトからの光が内部で混ざり合う。

Light from the peripheral openings, courtyard, and skylights blend together in the interior.

1200

0
Lux

June 12:00

1. ホール
   Hall
2. 展示ギャラリー
   Display gallery
3. 多目的活動室
   Multipurpose activity room

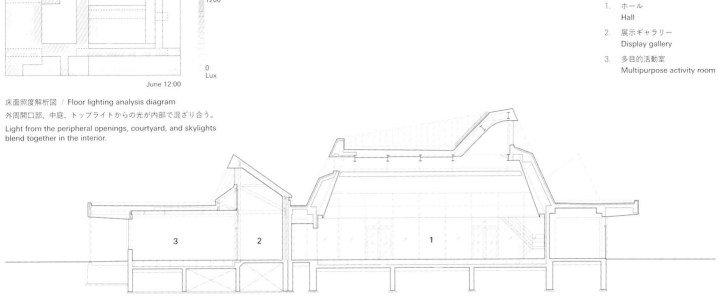

断面図 / Cross-section view  S=1:250

多目的活動室 / Multipurpose activity room

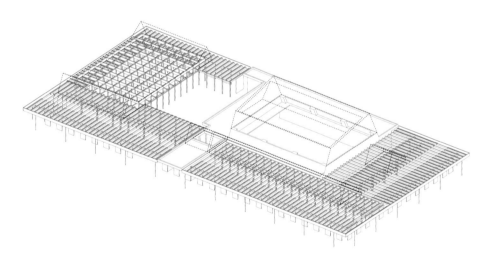

図書室 / Library

構造アクソメトリック / Structural isometric drawing

天井の高い図書室は、120mmの角材が1800mmピッチで並ぶ立体格子梁とした。図書室以外の部分は、短スパンの廊下と庇の間に7.2mの室が並ぶ構成を生かし、90 × 240mmの梁に120 × 240mmの梁を挟みこんだゲルバー梁とした。

The high-ceilinged library was designed with three-dimensional lattice beams using 120-mm square timbers lined up at a pitch of 1,800 mm. Other than the library, the rest of the structure was designed with Gerber beams using 120 x 240 mm beams in between 90 x 240 mm beams, in order to take advantage of the structure composed of 7.2-m rooms lined up between the short-span corridors and the eaves.

ゲルバー梁 / Gerber beams

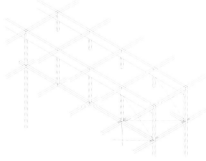

立体格子梁 / Three-dimensional lattice beams

RC造のホールを挟んで別棟とすることで全体の3分の2を木造としている。機能に応じて異なる架構形式を採用し、小中断面の道内産カラマツ材による親密な空間を実現した。

外壁の木造耐火壁は断熱性の向上に利用し、注意深く開口を設けて断熱気密性を確保した。外壁、ハイサイドライト、中庭からのそれぞれの光が混ざり合いながら内部では光の濃淡をつくる。厚い外皮に覆われた矩形平面の中で、木架構と自然光が奥行きのある空間をつくり、人々の活動が内側に展開する建築を目指した。

Two-thirds of the overall structure is made of wood, which was made possible by using separate buildings at opposite ends of the reinforced concrete hall. We adopted different frame types depending on the function, and achieved intimate spaces using Hokkaido-made Japanese larch wood with small to medium cross sections.

Wooden fireproof walls were used for the facade to improve heat insulation. Openings were carefully provided to ensure insulation and airtightness. Light from the outer walls, high sidelights, and courtyard coalesce to create light and shade inside. Wooden frames and natural light add depth to the space within a rectangular plan covered by a thick outer shell. We aimed for a building where people's activities develop inside.

# 上士幌町生涯学習センター わっか

Kamishihoro Lifelong Learning Center Wakka

—

2017

—

十勝地区北部の上士幌町において、まちなかに分散する学童保育、高齢者生きがいセンター等の公共施設を集約し、既存図書館と一体化する複合施設の計画である。既存施設機能を見直しながら複合化すると同時に、町民のくつろげる居場所を捻出した。周辺施設とのネットワークを形成することで「新たなまちの結節点」として機能することを目指した。

まちなかの結節点となるように出入口を四方向に設け、建物中央に配した円形の回遊動線につなげた。回遊動線に沿って活動が連続することで、様々な世代のふれあいを促す一体感が生まれる構成とした。

For Kamishihoro Town in the northern part of the Toka-chi District, the plan for the complex facility was to bring together public facilities such as the after-school childcare and senior citizen's life center, which were dispersed across the town, and integrate them with the existing library. While reviewing the functions of existing facilities, we worked out ideas for combining them while at the same time providing a relaxing place for the townspeople. We aimed for the building to function as a "new focal point for the town" by forming a network with surrounding facilities.

To serve as a focal point for the town, entryways are provided in four directions and are connected to the circular movement route arranged at the center of the building. A sense of unity is created in the structure through a series of activities conducted along the circular movement route, encouraging contact between various generations.

プレイルーム / Playroom

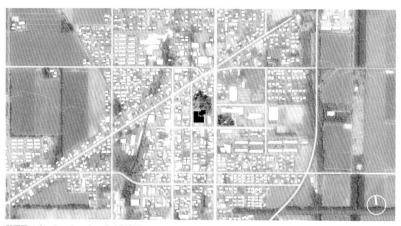

配置図 / Site location plan S=1:20000

計画地の四周に役場庁舎、こども園、商店街、住宅地等が隣接する。出入口を四方向に設けて町民の利便性を高めた。

On the four sides of the building site, the town hall building is adjacent to a childcare center, shopping district, and residential area, among others. Entryways are provided in four directions for the convenience of the townspeople.

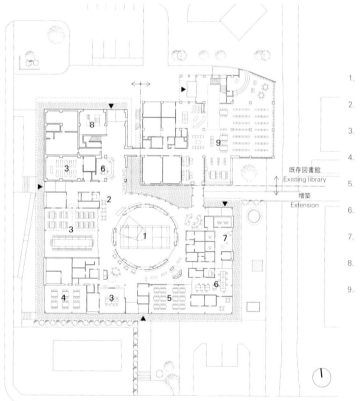

配置平面図 / Site floor plan S=1:1000

既存図書館
Existing library

増築
Extension

1. プレイルーム
   Playroom
2. プロムナード
   Promenade
3. 会議室
   Conference room
4. 陶芸室
   Pottery room
5. 学童保育室
   Children's nursery room
6. 事務室
   Office
7. 発達支援室
   Child development support room
8. 調理室
   Kitchen
9. 既存図書館
   Existing library

南鳥瞰 / Aerial view from the south

52

プロムナードからプレイルームを見る。
View of the playroom from the promnade.

1. プレイルーム
   Playroom
2. プロムナード
   Promenade
3. 既存図書館
   Existing library
4. 中庭
   Courtyard

奥行きの深い平面計画であるが、プレイルーム上部の中空ポリカーボネイトパネルによる拡散光、各所に設けた小さなハイサイドライト、中庭からの間接光等により、内部空間全体に自然光が行き渡るように計画した。
十分な自然光で満たされる開放的な木造建築の中で、町民の自由な活動が生まれる場所となることを目指した。

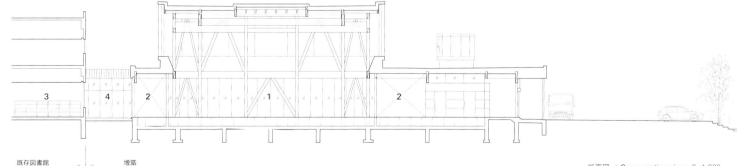

既存図書館
Existing library

増築
Extension

断面図 / Cross-section view  S=1:300

Although the floor plan has depth, we designed the building so that natural light spreads throughout the entire interior space, using diffused light from hollow polycarbonate panels above the playroom, small, high sidelights installed at various places, and indirect light from the courtyard.

We aimed for a place where all kinds of activities by the townspeople can be conceived in an open-plan wooden building adequately filled with natural light.

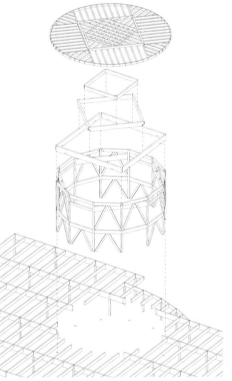

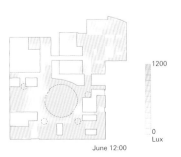

1200

0
Lux

June 12:00

床面照度解析図 / Floor lighting analysis diagram

直径18mのプレイルームは、円形平面を生かした梁を井桁状に架け渡す構造形式により、梁成を小さくし、材積を抑えながら大きな空間を実現した。

The 18-m diameter playroom creates a large space with a small beam configuration and low volume of materials through the adoption of a beam structure laid out in a grid-like pattern, which makes full use of the circular plan.

構造アイソメトリック / Structural isometric drawing

# 黒松内町庁舎耐震改修・
## コミュニティ防災センター

Kuromatsunai Town Hall Renovation /
Community Disaster Prevention Center

—

2015

—

築50年以上になる役場庁舎の大規模改修（耐震・断熱性向上）と防災センターの増築である。既存庁舎のRC躯体及び木造の小屋組を残すことを与条件に、全体の機能性を高める計画とした。
外部は既存庁舎の小屋組に基づく6寸勾配の濃緑板金屋根とレンガ壁を新築部にも採用し、庇や連窓などのディテールを統一した。既存の面影を残しながらも、もともと初めからこのようなかたちでつくられたかのような佇まいを目指した。

This project involves the large-scale renovation (seismic retrofitting and improvement of heat insulation) of a town hall that had stood for more than 50 years, as well as the addition of a building extension for the Disaster Prevention Center. Under the design condition that the reinforced concrete frame and wooden roof truss of the existing building be kept, we made plans to enhance overall functionality.
For the exterior, we adopted the same dark green sheet metal roof with 6/10 pitch of the existing building's roof truss and brick walls for the new construction, as well as matched their detailing, such as the eaves and continuous windows. While retaining the building's original features, we aimed for a look that suggests it was designed and constructed in this form from the very beginning.

配置図 / Site location plan  S=1:20000

東外観 / East facade

北外観 / North facade

1. 執務室
   Office
2. 議場
   Assembly hall
3. 風のみち
   Kaze no Michi
4. 町民談話室
   Community lounge

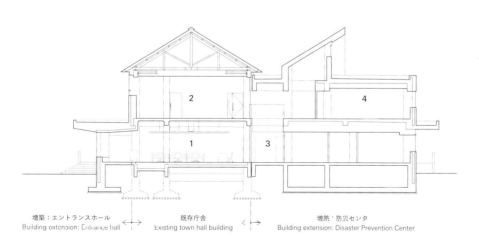

増築：エントランスホール
Building extension: Entrance hall

既存庁舎
Existing town hall building

増築：防災センタ
Building extension: Disaster Prevention Center

断面図 / Cross-section view　S=1:300

風のみち。左に既存躯体 / Kaze no Michi. Existing frame on the left

改修ダイアグラム / Renovation diagram

既存庁舎の小屋組に基づく6寸勾配の濃緑板金屋根と、レンガ壁を
新旧同じデザイン手法で採用した。

We adopted the same design technique for the old and new
sections, using a dark green sheet metal roof with 6/10 pitch of
the existing building's roof truss and brick walls.

既存庁舎躯体 / Existing town hall frame

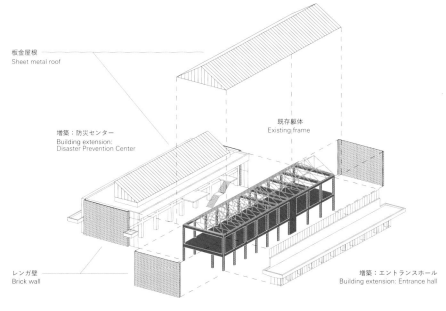

板金屋根
Sheet metal roof

増築：防災センター
Building extension:
Disaster Prevention Center

既存躯体
Existing frame

レンガ壁
Brick wall

増築：エントランスホール
Building extension: Entrance hall

執務室。新旧躯体の取合い
Office. Connection between old and new frames

南西外観 / Southwest facade

# 広域分散社会のシェルターの行方

岩澤浩一

## 「積雪寒冷」×「広域分散」

　近年のBNKの作品群から「積雪寒冷」と「広域分散」という二つの地域特性への複合的な取り組みが読み取れる。すなわち気候と社会構造である。気候的特性である「積雪寒冷」に対しては『Atelier BNK 2000-2014』の論考「亜寒帯のシェルター」で示された〈閉じながら開くシェルター〉、〈柔らかい光で満たされた空間〉、〈開拓地の風景〉といった三つの理念が基盤となりBNKの作品群を力強く支えている。一方、社会構造的特性である「広域分散」による地方自治体の財政問題や人口減少による公共施設群の再編、学校の統廃合や義務教育学校への移行、農地の再編など社会構造の変化に建築で如何に応えていくか。長く北海道の公共建築をリードしてきたBNKはこれら地域社会の課題に対して最前線で向かい合い、建築で応え続けてきた。少なからずBNKの作品を通して北海道という地域の現在が見えるといった構図が存在する。近年、この「広域分散」への建築的応答がBNKの作品群に新たな多様性を生み出す外在的な要因になっているのではないだろうか。いくつか具体的な作品に触れながら所感を述べてみたい。

## 夕張市拠点複合施設 りすた（2019）は、分散する公共施設群をコンパクトにまとめた「小さなまち」のような複合施設である。南側のバスターミナルに対しては東西に長い庇とガラススクリーンで大きく開き、北側の森にフォーカスするような台形の平面構成が特徴的である。南面に向けた東西に長いハイサイドライトは、奥行きの深い平面に程よく光を導き入れるよう、鉄骨の屋根架構の下の木ルーバーで光を拡散させている。「小さなまち」を空間化するために内部に中心性をつくらないように平面構成、視線の展開性、コントラストの弱い光分布が注意深く計画されている。近年木造の低層建築を数多く手がけているBNKであるが、この建物では鉄骨造が選択されており木ルーバーに鉄骨の屋根架構を潜ませるなど架構の存在感を弱めていることも開放的な空間の実現に寄与している。

## 上士幌町生涯学習センター わっか（2017）は、分散する公共施設群を集約し、既存図書館に増築するプロジェクトである。円形のプレイルームを中心としたL型の増築部分と既存図書館を2本の渡り廊下でつなぎ、新旧の建物を「プロムナード」と呼ばれる回遊動線でつなげる平面構成が特徴である。増築部分と既存図書館の間に生まれた隙間（外部空間）に差し込んだ光は既存図書館の外壁が反射面となり北側の「プロムナード」へ導き入れられる仕組みになっており、単に機能的な集約ではなく新旧の建物の相互作用によって「新たなまちの結節点」をつくることが意図されている。

## テクノロジーファーム 西の里（2018）は、農作物の防除作業に用いる農業用無人ヘリの保管、整備及び新しい農業技術の開発、実験の拠点である。北海道の農地は広大であることに加えて高齢化、後継者不足、耕作放棄地の増加など北海道を支える産業である農業は多くの課題を抱えており、新しい農業技術の開発が広域に分散する農地を維持するために不可欠となってきた。三つのウイングにより試験農場、試験水田、国道沿いの庭園を分けると同時に遠くに広がる札幌市の街並みや札幌ドーム、北広島に建設中のボールパークを望むダイナミックな形態は、新しい開拓地の風景を予感させる。

　これらの作品から「広域分散」への建築的応答においては、まちの人々や周辺環境と親密な関係を築く「開放性」、既存建築物と新築建築物の「相互性」、既存のビルディングタイプに捉われない「柔軟性」を備えたシェルターのビジョンが示されていると感じた。

## 60周年に向けて

　BNKの作品群に通底する建築としての質の高さは、50年を超える歴史と建築家たちの協同の中でつくられてきた作品群の弛まぬ実験と検証によって地層のように築き上げられてきたものだと感得する。8年後再び作品集がつくられるならば2030年。創設60周年にあたる年である。60年の歴史に向かって進む建築家集団は、その先の未来にとってかけがえのない存在である。次のマイルストーンとして「広域分散社会のシェルター」はどのように描かれていくのだろうか。多様な個性を内包した建築家集団であるBNKが建築の力で北海道の未来をどう切り開くのか、引き続き注目していきたい。

**岩澤浩一**（いわさわ こういち）
建築家／北海道科学大学准教授

1978年北海道生まれ。北海道工業大学大学院建築工学専攻修士課程修了後、2003年山本理顕設計工場入社。2009年id一級建築士事務所設立、iwasawa designに改組。東京理科大学工学部建築学科助教を経て現職。代表作に「河畔の家」「長泉の住宅」「望星病院」など。

# The Future of Shelters in Widely Decentralized Communities

Koichi IWASAWA

## Cold and snow & wide decentralization

Looking at the recent works of BNK, we can see their combined efforts to address two characteristics of the region—"cold and snow" and "wide decentralization." In other words, the climate and the social structure. For the climatic characteristics of "cold and snow," BNK's work portfolio has been strongly grounded on three core principles presented in the essay "Shelters in the Subarctic" in "Atelier BNK 2000–2014": "closed yet open shelters," "spaces filled with soft light," and "frontier landscape." Meanwhile, how can architecture adapt to changes in the social structure, such as financial problems in local governments caused by the social structure's characteristic "wide decentralization," reorganizations in public institutions caused by population decline, the abolition and consolidation of schools and the transition to schools for compulsory education, and the restructuring of farmlands? BNK has long been taking the lead in public building architecture in Hokkaido and has kept on addressing these local societal issues at the cutting edge through architecture. To a considerable extent, the current composition of the Hokkaido region can be observed through BNK's works. Their architectural response to this "wide decentralization" in recent years has likely become an extrinsic factor that has given rise to new diversity in BNK's works. I would like to discuss my impressions while mentioning a few specific works.

**Yubari City Community Base Complex RESTA (2019)** is a public facility complex similar to a "compact city" that compactly brings together decentralized groups of public facilities. The bus terminal at the south side is wide open with long eaves and glass screens from east to west, and is characterized by a trapezoidal planar configuration that places the focus on the forest at the north side. The high sidelights stretching east to west and facing southward diffuse light using wooden louvers under the steel roof frame to allow light to flow in moderation into the deep planar structure. To spatially create a "compact city," the planar configuration, extended line of sight, and low-contrast light distribution had been carefully planned so as not to create centrality inside. BNK has recently been working on a large number of low-rise wooden buildings, and while a steel frame structure was selected for this building, the frame's presence was soft-

ened by techniques such as concealing the steel roof framework with wooden louvers, contributing to the creation of an open space.

**Kamishihoro Lifelong Learning Center Wakka (2017)** is a project that brings together a group of decentralized public facilities and builds an extension to the existing library. It features an L-shaped building extension with a circular playroom at the center, which is connected by two corridors to the existing library. In the plan, the old and new buildings are joined by circulating movement routes called the "promenade." It was designed so that the existing library's facade becomes a reflective surface that guides the light entering the gap (external space) created between the building extension and the existing library into the promenade on the north side. Beyond merely consolidating various functions, the plan was to create a "new focal point for the town" through interaction between the old and new buildings.

**TECHNOLOGY FARM Nishinosato (2018)** is a center for the storage and maintenance of unmanned agricultural helicopters used for pest control of crops, as well as for the development and testing of new agricultural technologies. Aside from the vastness of agricultural lands in Hokkaido, agriculture as a vital industry in Hokkaido faces plenty of challenges, such as an aging population, lack of successors, and increasing number of abandoned farmlands. Developing new agricultural technologies is becoming indispensable to maintaining farmlands distributed over wide areas. The dynamic form lent by the three wings, which divide the test farm, test paddy field, and garden running along the national highway, and which at the same time overlook the faraway cityscape of Sapporo City, Sapporo Dome, and the ballpark under construction in Kitahiroshima, evokes a new frontier landscape.

Looking at these works, I believe that their architectural response to "wide decentralization" shows their vision for shelters providing openness to build intimate relationships with the people in the community and the surroundings, interaction between new and existing buildings, and flexibility that is not bound by the types of existing buildings.

## Toward its 60th anniversary

The high architectural quality that runs through BNK's works has been built up like geological layers—through tireless testing and verification of their works created in collaboration with architects across more than 50 years of history. If a collection of works is made again after eight years, the next one would be in 2030. That year would mark the 60th anniversary of BNK's founding. A team of architects moving toward 60 years of history is an irreplaceable treasure for the future. On the next milestone, I look forward to the depiction of "shelters in widely decentralized communities." I'll be eagerly waiting to see how BNK—a team of architects made up of diverse personalities—blazes a trail into the future of Hokkaido using the power of architecture.

Koichi IWASAWA
Architect, Associate Professor at Hokkaido University of Science

Born in Hokkaido in 1978. After graduating with a master's degree at the Graduate School of Architecture and Engineering, Hokkaido Institute of Technology, he joined Riken Yamamoto & Field Shop in 2003. He established id First-Class Architect's Office in 2009, later renamed iwasawa design. He assumed his current position after working as Assistant Professor at the Faculty of Engineering, Tokyo University of Science. His major works include House by the Riverside, Nagaizumi Residence, and Bosei Hospital.

# 北海道札幌視覚支援学校

Hokkaido Sapporo Special Needs
School for the Visually Impaired

—

2015

—

視覚障がいのある人を対象とした特別支援学校である。幼稚部から小学部、中学部、高等部（普通科・専攻科）まで、幅広い年齢層が学ぶ場であり、生活の場となる寄宿舎や、理療研修センターと併せて、一体的に整備することが求められた。住宅街に面する外周側は、複数の棟をひとつの外形輪郭に収めることで、統一感のある整った景観をつくりたいと考えた。一方、内側は棟と棟との間に生まれる不定形な中庭を場所ごとにつくり込み、多様でありながら安全な守られた屋外環境を創出することを試みた。

This project is for a special needs school for the visually impaired. The building provides a place of study for a wide range of age groups, from kindergarten to elementary school, junior high school, and high school (regular course/advanced course), and was required to be developed integrally and together with the living quarters—the school dormitory—and the physical therapy training center. On the outer periphery facing the residential area, we wanted to create a landscape with a sense of unity and order by putting together several buildings to form a single contour line. On the inside, however, we tried to create diverse yet safe and protected outdoor environments, using the irregularly shaped courtyards generated between buildings.

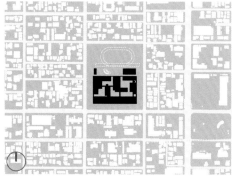

配置図 / Site location plan  S=1:10000

南西鳥瞰 / Aerial view from the southwest

雪が接することを考慮し、1階の窓下のみ外壁をコンクリート化粧打ち放しとした。外周側四周に庇を設けることで、寄宿舎玄関から校舎昇降口までの安全な移動を確保しながら、歩行訓練ルートとしても活用できるようにした。外と内の対比を強調するため、外周側は連窓／外壁フラット形状、内側は単窓／外壁角波形状と立面構成を変えている。

Taking contact with snow into account, an exposed concrete finish was used for the outer wall only under the windows on the first floor. Also, by providing eaves on the four peripheral sides, the building perimeter can be used as a training route for walking while also ensuring safe movement from the dormitory main entrance to the entrance of the school building. To emphasize the contrast between the outside and the inside, the composition of the building elevation is varied using continuous windows/flat outer walls on the outside perimeter and single windows/corrugated outer walls on the inside.

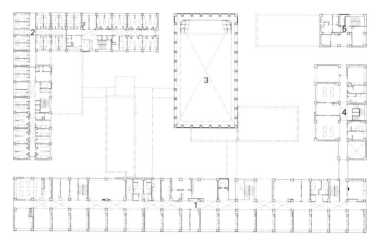

3階平面図 / Third floor plan

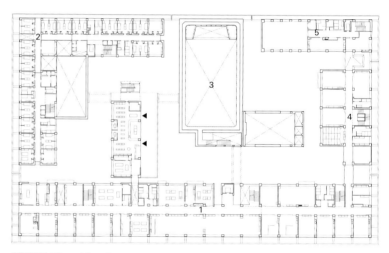

2階平面図 / Second floor plan

北東外観 / Northeast facade

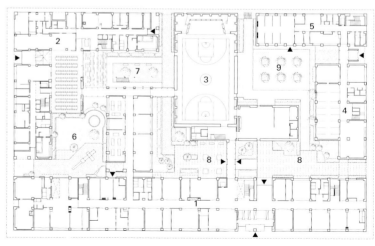

1階平面図 / First floor plan S=1:1200

北東外観 / Northeast facade

1. 校舎棟
   School building
2. 寄宿舎棟
   Dormitory building
3. 体育館棟
   Gymnasium building
4. 専攻課棟
   Advanced course building
5. 理療研修センター
   Physical therapy training center
6. 遊びの庭
   Garden of Play
7. 光の庭
   Garden of Light
8. 香りの庭
   Garden of Scents
9. 彩りの庭
   Garden of Color

彩りの庭 / Garden of Color

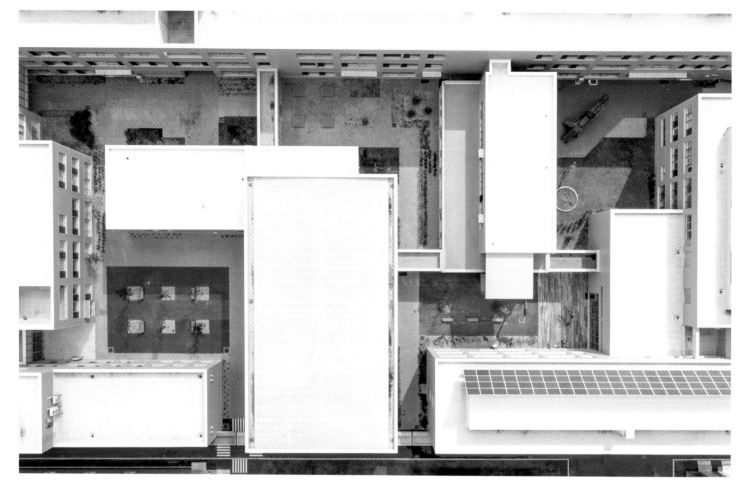

鳥瞰 / Aerial view

ランチルーム。奥に光の庭 / Lunchroom. The Garden of Light is at the back

体育館 / Gymnasium

香りの庭 / Garden of scents

# 利尻小学校・鬼脇中学校

Rishiri Elementary School /
Oniwaki Junior High School

——

2018

——

北海道北部の利尻島において、小学校と中学校を併置させる計画である。利尻富士の麓、港まで望むまちの高台に位置する傾斜地に、周辺の自然環境に呼応しながら、子どもたちが9年間通う居場所となる学校を計画した。

山とまちと海を結ぶ軸線上に、3つの矩形が連続したボリュームを配置し、小学校、中学校、体育館を分節しつつ共存させた。雁行した形状に併せて四周に窓を設け、風景と建築が見え隠れするシークエンスを体感できる。

For Rishiri Island in northern Hokkaido, the plan was to bring together an elementary school and a junior high school. Standing on a slope located on a hill overlooking the harbor at the foot of Rishiri-Fuji, we designed the school to be compatible with its natural surroundings while serving as a place for children to attend nine years of schooling.

On the line of axis connecting the mountain, the town, and the sea, we arranged a series of three rectangular volumes to segmentalize the elementary school, junior high school, and gymnasium, while at the same time allowing them to coexist together. Windows are provided on all four sides to match the echelon formation of the structure and to allow for experiencing the sequence of appearing and disappearing landscape and architectural views.

北鳥瞰 / Aerial view from the north

配置図 / Site location plan　S=1:10000

山とまちと海を結ぶ軸線に沿った傾斜地に位置する。
雁行した形状は高い木々に囲われた不整形で狭小な空間に対して造
成を最小限にする。

Located on a slope along the axis connecting the mountain, the
town, and the sea.
The echelon formation minimizes land preparation for the
irregularly shaped and narrow space covered by tall trees.

南外観 / South facade

1階平面図 / First floor plan S=1:1000

2階平面図 / Second floor plan

1. エントランスホール
   Entrance hall
2. 図書メディアコーナー
   Library media corner
3. 小中交流スペース
   Elementary and junior
   high socializing area
4. 小学校普通教室
   Elementary school regular
   classroom
5. 特別教室
   Special classroom
6. 体育館
   Gymnasium
7. 職員室
   Staff room
8. 児童会・生徒会室
   Elementary and junior high
   student council room
9. 中学校普通教室
   Junior high school regular
   classroom

2階廊下 / Second floor hallway

連続する小さなループ動線の四周に教室やオープンスペースを点在させ、小学校、中学校のそれぞれの教育環境の確保と諸室の共有を両立させる適切な距離感をつくり出した。小さな空間が連続する平面は複式学級や個別学習等の小規模校特有の教育状況にも対応している。風雪や塩害が厳しいため、耐候性の高い素材の外断熱工法で建物を覆った。内部では階高を低く抑え、コンクリートの量塊が空間をかたちづくる。制約の多い離島の建築として、建設や維持管理が容易な汎用的工法で構築した。

We distributed classrooms and open spaces around the perimeter of the series of small pathway loops to create a suitable sense of distance that balances the need for securing an educational environment separately for the elementary school and junior high school, and for sharing various rooms. The plan, composed of a series of small spaces, accommodates the unique educational situation of small schools, such as combined classes for more than one grade level and individual learning.

Because of severe wind and snow as well as salt damage, the building is covered with outer insulation made of high-performance weatherproof material. Inside, floor heights are kept low, with concrete masses creating forms for the space. For a building on a remote island with many restrictions, it was built with a general construction method for easy construction and maintenance.

2階エントランスホール / Second floor entrance hall

1階エントランスホール / First floor entrance hall

# 名寄南小学校

Nayoro Minami Elementary School

—

2016

—

コンパクト化を徹底し、体育館の四周を3層の校舎が完全に取り囲む構成とした小学校である。採光の取れない体育館と廊下との間にトップライトを設けた3層吹抜空間を挿入し、光と風の通り道とした。体育館の2階レベル以上の壁はガラスカーテンウォールとし、競技等に影響のない範囲で内側に倒すことで、吹抜空間の上部気積を拡大し効果的に光を取り込みながら、構造スパンの低減も図っている。体育館の通風は、屋上に換気用ハト小屋を設置し、地中に埋めたクール・ヒートチューブから給気することで、負荷軽減を図る計画とした。日々の活動を様々な場所から互いに見通すことができ、子どもたちにとって一体感のある学び舎となった。

This project is for a thoroughly compact elementary school with a gymnasium that is completely surrounded on all sides by a three-story school building. A three-story atrium space containing skylights is tucked in between the gymnasium where windows could not be installed and the hallways, to create passages for light and wind. We used glass curtain walls for walls above the second-floor level of the gymnasium. By inclining them inward up to a point that does not affect sports competitions and other considerations, we expanded the air volume at the upper part of the atrium space to effectively let light in while also reducing structural spans. For ventilation in the gymnasium, we planned to install roof vents at the rooftop and supply air from cooling and heating tubes buried underground to reduce loads. It became a school building with a sense of unity for the children, where they could see each other's day-to-day activities from various vantage points.

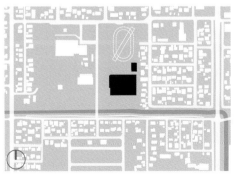

配置図 / Site location plan S=1:10000

体育館 / Gymnasium

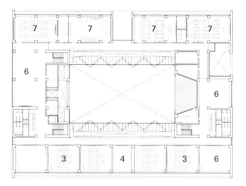

3階平面図 / Third floor plan

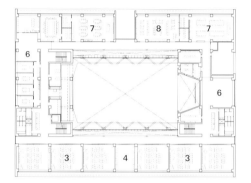

2階平面図 / Second floor plan

1階平面図 / First floor plan　S=1:1200

体育館 / Gymnasium

1.　職員室
　　Staff room

2.　体育館
　　Gymnasium

3.　普通教室
　　Regular classroom

4.　ワークスペース
　　Work space

5.　特別支援教室
　　Special needs classroom

6.　プレイルーム
　　Playroom

7.　多目的教室
　　Multipurpose classroom

8.　図書室
　　Library

西外観 / West facade

3階普通教室 / Third floor class room

吹抜空間 / Atrium

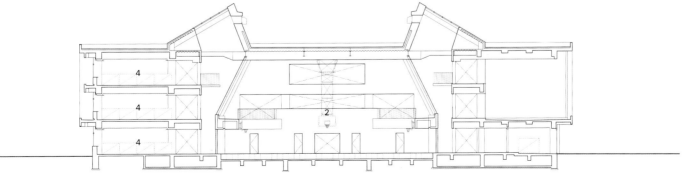

断面図 / Cross-section view  S=1:400

# 開西中学校

Kaisei Junior High School

—

2015

—

老朽化が進み一部耐震性能が不足する校舎・体育館におい
て、RC造校舎は耐震改修＋大規模改修、CB造校舎と体育館
は解体の上新築という複雑なプログラムを遂行したプロジェ
クトである。最終形としては、体育館に校舎がL字に取り付
くコンパクトな構成とし、既存棟と新築棟とが面する部分に
は「開西スクエア」と名付けた3層吹抜のアトリウム空間を挿
入した。ガラス屋根から降り注ぐ自然光が、古い壁面と新し
い壁面を対比させながら、絶えず生徒が行き交い滞留する学
校の中心的な交流の場を生み出している。

For the school building and gymnasium which had deteriorated
with age and been confirmed to have insufficient seismic performance in some areas, the project involved carrying out a compli-
cated program of seismic retrofitting and large-scale renovation
for the reinforced concrete school building, as well as the demolition of the concrete block school building and gymnasium and
building new replacements. The final form is a compact configuration, with the school building attached to the gymnasium in an
L-shaped structure. A three-story atrium space called "Kaisei
Square" is integrated into the section where the existing building
and the new building face each other. Natural light shines down
from the glass roof to produce contrasts between the old and new
walls, creating a central meeting place for the school where students can continually mingle and stay.

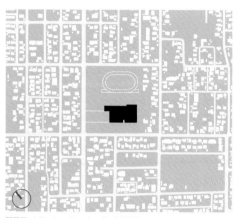

配置図 / Site location plan S=1:10000

開西スクエア / Kaisei Square

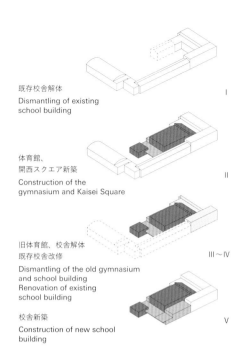

既存校舎解体
Dismantling of existing
school building

I

体育館、
開西スクエア新築
Construction of the
gymnasium and Kaisei Square

II

旧体育館、校舎解体
既存校舎改修
Dismantling of the old gymnasium
and school building
Renovation of existing
school building

III〜IV

校舎新築
Construction of new school
building

V

改修ダイアグラム / Renovation diagram
解体、改築、改修の各工事と引越しが絡む工事プログラムを、
フェーズ I 〜 V に整理し、空き教室を有効活用することで仮設
校舎を設けずに、約2年に渡る使いながらの工事を実現している。

The construction program was organized into Phases 1 to 5,
which involved various works — from demolition to
rebuilding to renovating as well as moving. Through the
effective use of vacant classrooms, we were able to carry
out the construction for about two years while using the
facilities without installing a temporary school building.

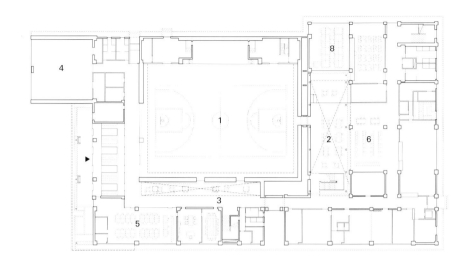

1階平面図 / First floor plan  S=1:800

1. 体育館
   Gymnasium

2. 開西スクエア
   Kaisei Square

3. ときのみち
   Toki no Michi

4. 武道場
   Martial arts hall

5. 職員室
   Staff room

6. 図書室
   Library

7. 普通教室
   Regular classroom

8. 特別教室
   Special classroom

開西スクエア / Kaisei square

西外観 / West facade

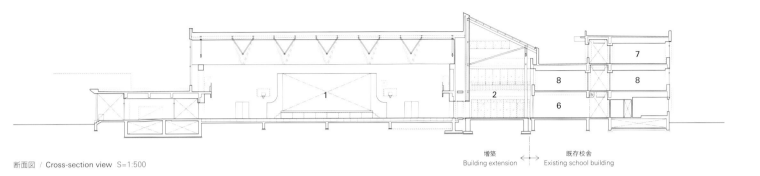

断面図 / Cross-section view S=1:500

増築　←→　既存校舎
Building extension　Existing school building

体育館と新築校舎の間に小さな2層吹抜空間をつくり、壁面に旧校舎の歴史や思い出を展示した「ときのみち」として設えた。

外観としては、地域住民に親しまれていた旧校舎の赤い板金屋根を、体育館の外壁を包むカラーガルバリウム角波鋼板に移し変えた。校舎のコンパクト化により生まれたアプローチ前庭は、イベント等に活用できる広場として利用されている。

We also created a small two-story atrium space between the gymnasium and the newly built school building, where we set up Toki no Michi (the passage of time), a display of the history and mementos of the old school building on the walls.

For the facade, the red sheet metal roof of the old school building, which had been a familiar sight to local residents, was transformed into colored Galvalume square corrugated steel sheets that cover the outer walls of the gymnasium. The vast front garden approach created by downsizing the school building is utilized as a plaza that can be used for events.

ときのみち / Toki no Michi

## 厚沢部町認定こども園 はぜる

Assabu Center for Early Childhood Hazeru
Education and Care

—

2018

—

築50年を迎えた3つの保育所を統合し、町内唯一となる認定こども園をつくるプロジェクトである。厚沢部は、江戸時代から林業を生業としている町であり、この豊かな町産木材の活用を与条件に木造在来工法で計画を進めた。敷地は山の裾野にあり、土地の高低差があることで南面保育室のテラス、アプローチの大階段がつくられた。全体の高さを抑えた外観は2階建のイエをコレクトした佇まいでひとりひとりの居場所であることを示唆しつつ、背景の山々に溶けこむような印象を与える。

This project merges three nursery schools that had been around for 50 years and creates the only certified center for early childhood education and care in the town. Assabu is a town that has been in the forestry business since the Edo period. We worked on a plan that employs a conventional wooden construction method under the condition that the town's abundant timber is used. The site is located at the foot of a mountain. Because of the differences in elevation of the land, we created a terrace at the nursery room on the south side and a large stairway at the approach. For the facade, we minimized the overall building height to suggest a place where each person can feel a sense of belonging through the image of a collection of two-story homes, and to give the impression of blending with the mountains in the background.

配置図 / Site location plan  S=1:15000

1.  子育て支援センター
    Childcare support center

2.  絵本のまちあいホール
    Waiting hall with picture books

3.  職員室
    Staff room

4.  ステージ / 午睡室
    Stage / Nap room

5.  遊戯室
    Playroom

6.  保育室
    Nursery room

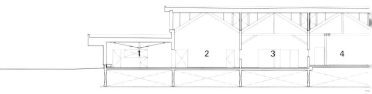

南外観 / South facade

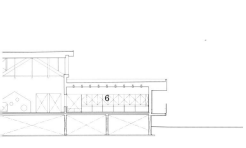

断面図 / Cross-section view　S=1:400

西外観 / West facade

平面は、職員室、遊戯室を中心にそれらを取り巻くように
保育室やバックスペースを配し、回遊動線で接続されてい
る。東西南北すべての方角にハイサイドライトを設けた高
さ5.8mの吹抜が職員室と遊戯室、各室をつなぐ動線を覆
い、外周部各室の二面採光を可能にすると同時に、1日の
大半を過ごす子どもたちに光の移ろいをもたらす。

The plan distributes nursery rooms and back spaces around the
staff room and playroom, which are all connected by a circular
movement path. A 5.8-m high atrium with high sidelights in all
directions, north, south, east, and west, encompasses the staff
room, the playroom, and the movement path connecting each
room, which makes it possible to capture daylight from two
sides of each room on the outer circumference, and at the same
time bring the changing lights to the children who spend most
of their day here.

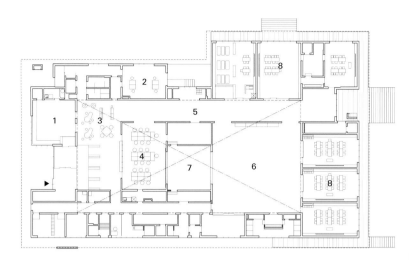

平面図 / Floor plan S=1:600

| | | | |
|---|---|---|---|
| 1. | 子育て支援センター<br>Childcare support center | 5. | 大きな廊下<br>Large hallway |
| 2. | 発達支援室<br>Child development support room | 6. | 遊戯室<br>Playroom |
| 3. | 絵本のまちあいホール<br>Wating hall with picture books | 7. | ステージ / 午睡室<br>Stage / Nap room |
| 4. | 職員室<br>Staff room | 8. | 保育室<br>Nuesery room |

絵本のまちあいホール / Waiting hall with picture books

大きな廊下 / Large hallway

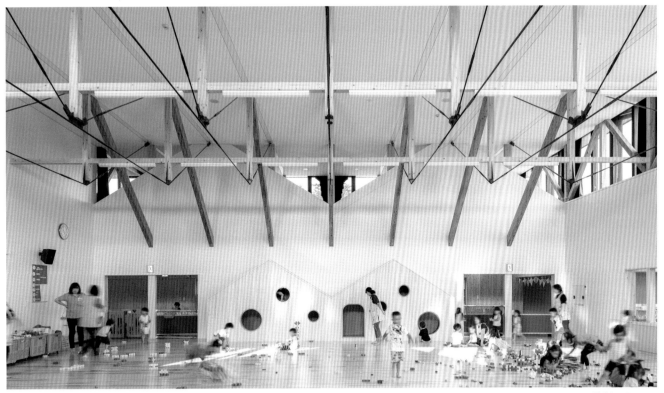

遊戯室 / Playroom

遊戯室から保育室を見る。
View of the nursery room from the playroom.

85

# 北星学園大学
# キャンパスリノベーション

Hokusei Gakuen University
Campus Renovation

—

2015

—

開学50周年を節目に教育環境の向上と交流の場の充実などを目的とした、札幌市内の大学キャンパスのリノベーション計画である。

施設群の新しい核となる新C館建設のほか、既存校舎や外構を部分的に改修することで、キャンパス全体の機能向上とイメージアップを目指した。既存キャンパスは緑あふれる美しい中庭を核とした施設配置がなされており、この中庭との関係を重視すること、加えて調和のとれた現施設群の中にいくつかの痕跡を加えることで、総体としての新しい風景をつくり出すことがテーマである。学生たちが大学の歴史の重みを感じる場所であってほしいと願っている。

Marking the 50th anniversary of the university's founding, this project is for the renovation of the university campus in Sapporo City to improve the educational environment and provide a richer place for social interaction. Aside from the construction of the new Building C, the new core of a group of facilities, we aimed to improve the image and functionalities of the entire campus by partially renovating existing school buildings and external structures. The existing campus had facilities arranged around a beautiful verdant courtyard. The theme is to create a new landscape as a whole, by emphasizing the relationship with this courtyard as well as by adding a few harmonious signatures among the current facilities. We hope that this provides a place where students can feel the weight of the university's history.

ホワイエから中庭を見る / View of the courtyard from the foyer

| | | |
|---|---|---|
| a. | チャペル<br>Chapel | 1964 |
| b1. | 大学会館<br>College Hall | 1986 |
| b2. | 第一研究棟<br>Faculty Office Building 1 | 1986 |
| b3. | サークル会館<br>Student Activities Building | 1986 |
| c. | 図書館棟<br>Library Building | 1990 |
| d. | B棟<br>Building B | 1996 |
| e. | 体育館<br>Gymnasium | 2000 |
| f1. | A-2棟<br>Building A-2 | 2001 |
| f2. | 第二研究棟<br>Faculty Office Building 2 | 2001 |
| f3. | 大学会館（増築）<br>College Hall (extension) | 2001 |
| g. | 図書館棟（増築）<br>Library Building (extension) | 2003 |

| | | |
|---|---|---|
| 1. | 新C館（改築）<br>New Building C (reconstruction) | 1978 (2015) |
| 2. | A-1棟（改修）<br>Building A-1 (renovation) | 2001 (2015) |
| 3. | センター棟（改修）<br>Center Building (renovation) | 1981 (2015) |
| 4. | カバードウォーク<br>Covered walkway | 2015 |
| 5. | 守衛所<br>Guardhouse | 2015 |
| 6. | プロムナード<br>Promenade | 2015 |

配置図 / Site location plan S=1:2500

中庭を核として各年代に建設された施設群（上遠野徹によりキャンパス全体の計画と大部分の建築が設計された）で構成されるキャンパスにおいて、新C館はこの中庭との関係を重視しながら、これを囲うような配置計画とした。また、正門のアイストップとして新たな顔をつくり出すことを意図した。

In a campus consisting of clusters of facilities built in each decade around a central courtyard (the overall campus plan and most of the buildings were designed by Tetsu Katono), the new Building C has a layout plan that appears to surround this courtyard as it emphasizes its relationship with the courtyard. We also created an eye-catching new look for the Front Gate.

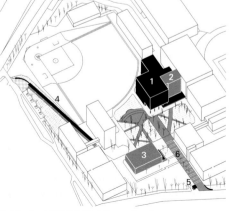

リノベーションダイアグラム / Renovation diagram

北門（新設）：門とカバードウォークを計画し、駅方向からの歩行者動線の機能向上を図った。

North Gate (new): We designed a gate and covered walkway to improve the pedestrian walkway functionality from the direction of the station.

88

正門（改修）：中庭へのプロムナードやチャペルで用いられている青色タイルで新たな門を整備し、キャンパスの顔として設え直しを図った。

Front Gate (renovation): A new gate was constructed using blue tiles, which were used in the chapel and the promenade to the courtyard. It was rebuilt to serve as the face of the campus.

センター棟（改修）：耐震補強及び内部全面改修。プロムナードに面するカフェや、アクティブラーニングスペース等を配している。

Center Building (renovation): Seismic retrofitting and full interior renovation. We provided a café facing the promenade and an active learning space, among others.

A-1館（改修）：新C館に隣接するA-1館はスケルトン改修を行い、外壁カーテンウォールによる中庭と市街地を望むラウンジ空間を設けた。

Building A-1 (renovation): Building A-1, which is adjacent to the new Building C, has undergone a skeleton renovation. A lounge space with a view of the courtyard and the city area was provided using a curtain wall facade.

1階平面図 / First floor plan S=1:1000

1. エントランスホール
   Entrance hall
2. ホワイエ
   Foyer
3. 大講堂
   Large auditorium
4. 事務室
   Office
5. 共同研究所
   Joint research laboratory
6. 事務室
   Office
7. 講義室
   Lecture room

2階ホワイエ / Second floor foyer

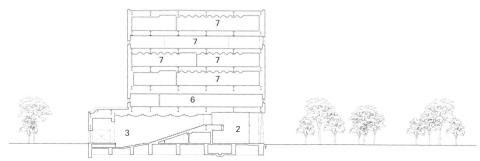

断面図 / Cross-section view S=1:800

大講堂 / Large auditorium

新C館は、1・2階に500人収容の大講堂（50周年記念ホール）とホワイエ、上階は講義室と事務機能をもつ。外壁には青色のタイル（既存学内チャペルから引用）と金属パネルを用い、キャンパスの基調である白色タイルと対比させた。隣接するA-1館は外壁をカーテンウォールに改修し、1階はエントランスホール、上の各階は中庭と市街地を望むラウンジ空間とした。

プロムナードのアイストップとなる本館は、キャンパスの新しいランドマークとなった。

The new Building C has a foyer and a large auditorium that seats 500 (50th Anniversary Hall) on the first and second floors, as well as lecture rooms and offices on the upper floors. For the facade, blue tiles (referred from the existing campus chapel) and metallic panels were used as a contrast to the white tiles, which are the keynote of the campus. The facade of the adjacent Building A-1 was renovated using curtain walls, with an entrance hall on the first floor and a lounge space with a view of the courtyard and city area on the upper floors.

This eye-catching building along the promenade has become a new landmark on campus.

西外観 / West facade

# 滝川市栄町3-3地区再開発事業

Takikawa City Sakae-Machi 3-3 District
Redevelopment Project

—

2018

—

北海道中空知の中心都市・滝川における再開発事業である。商業地区の中心である栄町3-3地区は、まちの核となる商業施設が閉店してから10年放置されてきた。その後、まちづくり会社が事業者を探し、代行型再開発事業が行われたのが本計画である。商業施設は敷地いっぱいに建てられていたが、医療介護施設、金融機関本店の2棟とオープンスペースから成る計画とした。敷地は国道と賑わいが失われた商店街に接しているが、周辺には市の中核施設が少なからず点在する。バス停、新たに設けた自転車置き場、駐車場、それらを結ぶカバードウォーク、大小の広場、雨や雪をしのぐロッジア、透明なギャラリーを街区に設け、賑わいが集まることを目指した。

This is a redevelopment project in Takikawa, a central city in Nakasorachi, Hokkaido. Sakae-Machi 3-3 District is at the center of a commercial district and had been neglected for 10 years since its core commercial facility closed. Consequently, the town development company searched for a business operator, resulting in this project, which was carried out as an agency-led redevelopment project. Although commercial facilities had been built to fill the site, the plan consists of two buildings—a medical and long-term care facility and the headquarters of a financial institution—and open spaces. The site is bordered by the national highway and a shopping district that has lost its vitality, although there are a number of core facilities of the city around the neighborhood. We provided the block with bus stops, newly installed bicycle parking areas, parking lots, covered walkways connecting them, plazas of different sizes, a loggia for taking shelter from the rain and snow, and a clear gallery, with the aim of attracting crowds to the area.

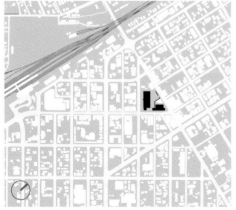

配置図 / Site location plan S=1:15000

南東外観 / Southeast facade

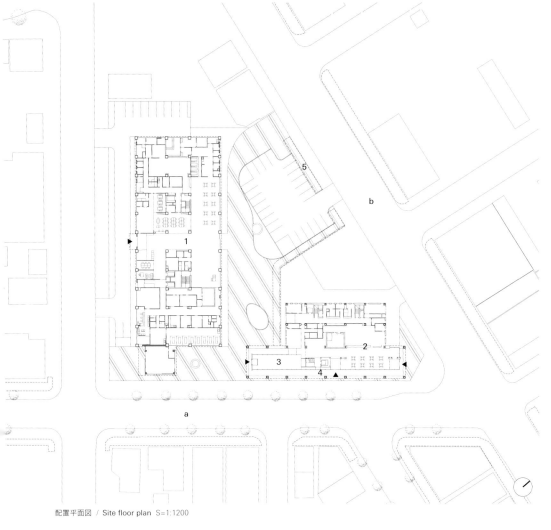

配置平面図 / Site floor plan  S=1:1200

1. 医療介護施設
   Medical and long-term
   care building
2. 金融機関
   Banking facility
3. ギャラリー
   Gallery
4. ロッジア
   Loggia
5. カバードウォーク
   Covered walkway

a. 商店街
   Shopping street
b. 国道
   National highway

北東外観 / Northeast facade

旧3-3地区商業施設 / Former 3-3 District commercial facility
敷地全体にわたって建てられていた旧商業施設に対し、今回計画では2棟に分割し、商店街と連続する空地を確保した。

The old commercial facility had been built across the entire site, while the current plan splits the site into two buildings in order to secure open spaces that link with the shopping district.

北西外観 / Northwest facade

金融機関 待合 / Waiting area of the banking facility

# テクノロジーファーム 西の里

## TECHNOLOGY FARM Nishinosato

2018

---

農業に関する幅広い事業を扱う企業が所有する農業用無人ヘリの保管・整備拠点である。札幌の郊外、都市と農村の結節点であるこの場所は、新しい農業技術の開発、実験を一貫して行うことができる場である。南側に広がる農地を3つのウイングが、試験農場、試験水田、国道沿線のための庭園に分節する。

This is a storage and maintenance center for unmanned agricultural helicopters, and is owned by a company that handles a wide range of agricultural businesses. The location is on a focal point between the city and rural areas in a suburb of Sapporo, and is a place where new agricultural technologies can be systematically developed and tested. The farmland spreading over the southern side is divided by three wings into a test farm, a test paddy field, and a garden bordering the national highway.

配置図 / Site location plan S=1:10000

西鳥瞰 / Aerial view from the west

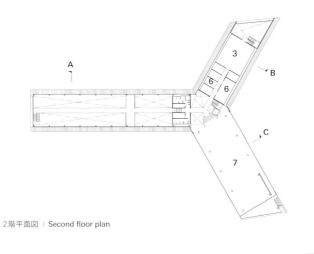

2階平面図 / Second floor plan

1. ホール
   Hall
2. 整備事務室
   Maintenance office
3. 格納庫
   Storage
4. 整備場
   Maintenance yard
5. 農機具庫
   Agricultural machinery and
   equipment storage
6. 精密部品庫
   Precision instruments storage
7. 屋内練習場
   Indoor practice field
a. 試験農場
   Test farm
b. 試験水田
   Test paddy field
c. 試験飛行地
   Test flight zone
d. 庭園
   Garden

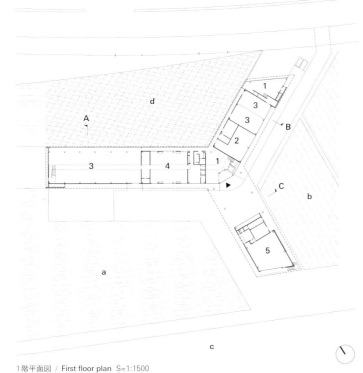

1階平面図 / First floor plan  S=1:1500

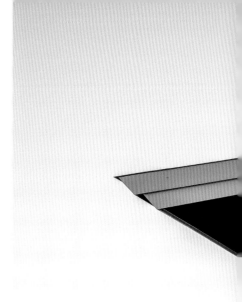

南外観 / South facade

三つのウイングは、門型と家型の二種類のフレームで構成され、階数の違い、ピロティの有無によってそれぞれの断面形をもつ。各ウイングの端部に階段を設けることで、中央のエントランスホールからすべてのウイングを横断する経路をつくり、異なる分野の交流を促す開発拠点となることを意図した。

北外観 / North facade

The three wings consist of two types of frames, a portal frame and a house-shaped frame, each with its own cross-sectional shape depending on the number of floors and on whether pilotis are used or not. By installing stairways at the end of each wing, we created routes that go across all the wings from the entrance hall at the center, with the intention of creating a development hub that encourages communication among the different fields.

北西外観 / Northwest facade

廊下 / Hallway

格納庫 / Storage

ホール / Hall

A

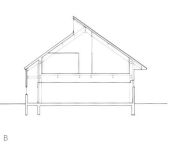

B

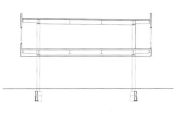

C

断面図 / Cross-section view　S＝1:500

格納庫 / Storage

# ウポポイ
## 体験交流ホール

Upopoy
Cultural Exchange Hall

—

2019

—

アイヌの歴史・文化の体験と交流をテーマとして伝統芸能などが上演される多目的ホールである。内部のステージ、客席は「借景軸」を中心にシンメトリーに構成し、ステージ背後の開口部からポロト湖の向こう、伝統的コタン（住居であるチセの集まり）に向かって焦点をつくる。断面形は1枚の大きな曲面屋根を傾斜させて架け、全体の気積を抑えながらステージ上に必要十分なスペースを確保した。内部客席はアイヌの古式舞踊の形式である輪踊りが映えるように、円形のスラスト型ステージのまわりに客席を配する構成とした。演者と観客が垣根を越えてひとつになり、ウポポイ（「おおぜいで歌うこと」の意）の名にふさわしい一体感のある空間を目指した。

This project is for a multipurpose hall for performing traditional performance arts and such under the theme of "experiencing and exchanging" Ainu history and culture. The interior stage and audience seats are symmetrically structured with an "axis of borrowed scenery" at the center. The opening at the back of the stage creates a focus toward Kotan (a group of dwellings called "cise"), the traditional Ainu village across Lake Poroto. The cross section was constructed with a single enormous curved roof that slants and hangs over the stage to provide the space that was necessary and sufficient while at the same time controlling the overall air volume. The interior audience seats are arranged around a circular thrust stage to attractively show the "circle dance"—a traditional Ainu dance. We aimed for a space where the performers and the audience can cross barriers and become one in a sense of unity that fits the name "Upopoy" (which means "singing together in a large group").

南東外観 / Southeast facade

配置図 / Site location plan  S=1:10000

a. ポロト湖
   Lake Poroto
b. チセ
   Cise
c. 国立アイヌ民族博物館
   National Ainu Museum
d. チキサニ広場
   Cikisani Square
e. 屋外ステージ
   Outdoor stage
f. 借景軸
   Axis of borrowed scenery

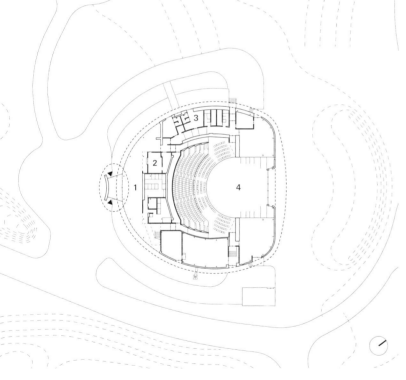

平面図 / Floor plan  S=1:1000

1. ホワイエ
   Foyer
2. 事務室
   Office
3. 楽屋
   Dressing room
4. ステージ
   Stage

断面図 / Cross-section view  S=1:1000

ポロト湖南端のほとりは、山の稜線と国立アイヌ民族博物館に囲われた平坦で見通しのよい場所である。ここに円形プランの変形からつくられたシリンダー状のかたちを置いた。曲面屋根は対岸の伝統的コタンに向かう「借景軸」に沿って勾配を付けた。

The southern shore of Lake Poroto is a flat, clear area surrounded by the National Ainu Museum and mountain ridges. A cylindrical shape made from deforming a circular plan was placed here. The curved roof was made to incline along an "axis of borrowed scenery" facing Kotan, the traditional Ainu village on the opposite shore.

ステージ / Stage

屋外ステージ / Outdoor stage

# 幌東病院

Koto Hospital

———

2017

———

札幌市郊外の240床の慢性期病院である。長期在院する患者が四季の変化を感じながら前向きな気分になり、元の生活に戻るイメージを持てる場となることを目指した。

敷地周辺は低層の住宅地であることから、建物高さを抑えた配置計画とした。1階は雪から守られた雁木、ピロティ空間を外周に回し、北側商店街や東側幹線道路とつながる関係をつくった。2、3階は、中庭を中心にした60床の病棟を二つ連結し、中庭を囲むように街路に面して病室を配置した。院内には、中庭や屋上テラス、ピロティなどの外気に触れる場所、これらと連続するラウンジ、デイルームなどの居場所を点在させ、患者が移動しながら季節の気配やまちの風景を感じることができる。

This project involved a 240-bed long-term care hospital in the suburbs of Sapporo City. We aimed to create a place in which patients who have been in the hospital for a long time can feel optimistic as they enjoy the four seasons, and which allows them to imagine returning to their everyday lives.

In the plan, we reduced the building height since the site is in a low-rise residential area. The first floor has pathways covered by deep eaves to protect from the snow and is surrounded at the periphery by pillared spaces. We created connections that link the shopping district to the north with the arterial road on the east side. On the second and third floors, two 60-bed wards are connected and built around a central courtyard, with the hospital rooms facing the streets. The hospital is interspersed with places to breath fresh air, such as the courtyard, roof terrace, and pillared spaces, as well as places leading to these, such as the lounge and day room, so that patients can sense the changing seasons and urban scenery while moving around.

北東外観 / Northeast facade

ラウンジ / Lounge
本郷通り商店街を望む空間。
A space overlooking the Hongo Shopping Street.

北外観 / North facade
本郷通り商店街と連続する街並みをつくる。
The facade creates a continuous streetscape with the Hongo Shopping Street.

配置図 / Site location plan　S=1:10000

２階廊下 / Second floor hallway
中庭からの自然光が病室に入り込む。
Natural light falls into the hospital room from the courtyard.

待合コーナー / Waiting corner

スタッフステーション / Staff station
病棟の中心である中庭に面する。
Facing the courtyard, which stands at the center of the hospital wards.

デイルーム / Day room

| | | | |
|---|---|---|---|
| 1. | エントランスロビー<br>Entrance lobby | 7. | 2床室<br>Two-bed room |
| 2. | 事務室<br>Office | 8. | 1床室<br>One-bed room |
| 3. | 診療室<br>Examination room | 9. | スタッフステーション<br>Staff station |
| 4. | ラウンジ<br>Lounge | 10. | デイルーム<br>Day room |
| 5. | 待合コーナー<br>Waiting corner | 11. | 中庭<br>Courtyard |
| 6. | 4床室<br>Four-bed room | 12. | 屋上テラス<br>Rooftop terrace |

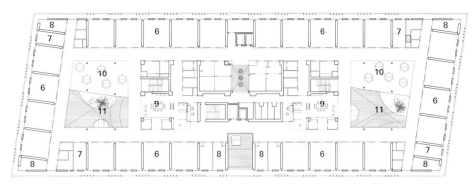

2階平面図 / Second floor plan

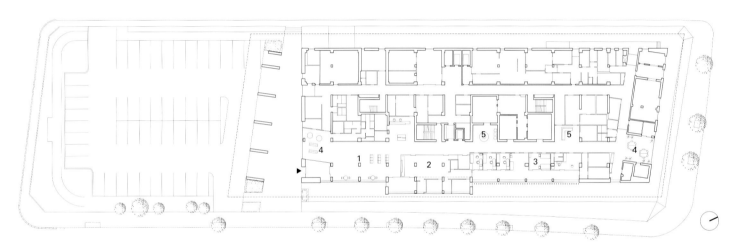

1階平面図 / First floor plan S=1:800

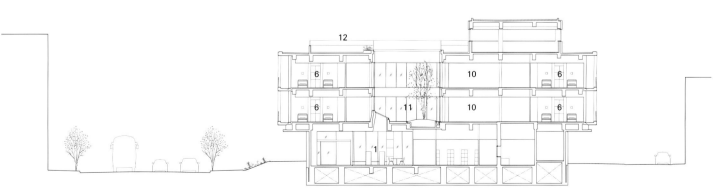

断面図 / Cross-section view S=1:400

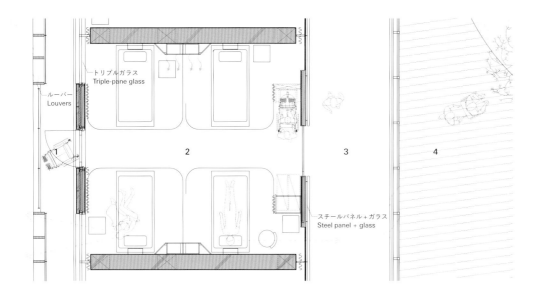

トリプルガラス
Triple-pane glass

ルーバー
Louvers

1    2    3    4

スチールパネル＋ガラス
Steel panel + glass

病室の縦スリット窓は、窓面積を抑えながら高い位置から十分な自然光を導く。トリプルガラスによる高断熱化を図った。廊下側の壁面はスチールとガラスの平滑な面で構成し、自然光を反射、拡散する。

Slit vertical windows in the room let in enough natural light from a high position while reducing window area. Good thermal insulation is achieved using triple-pane glass. Hallway-side walls are composed of smooth steel and glass surfaces to reflect and diffuse natural light.

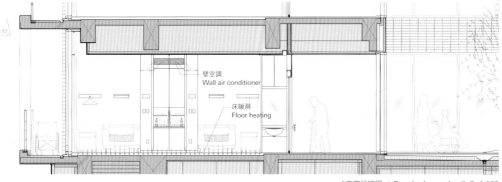

壁空調
Wall air conditioner

床暖房
Floor heating

4床室詳細図 / Four-bedroom detail  S=1:100

1.　バルコニー
　　Balcony

2.　病室
　　Hospital room

3.　廊下
　　Hallway

4.　中庭
　　Courtyard

廊下から見る病室 / Hospital room as seen from the hallway

4床室 / Four-bed room

一般的な4床室は、窓側ベッドと廊下側ベッドの居住性に大きな格差ができる。今回計画では廊下面に開口部を設け、中庭からの間接光を拡散させながら廊下側ベッドへと導いた。一方窓側ベッドでは、バルコニーと縦ルーバーを組み合わせて日射遮蔽とプライバシー確保を行った。このバルコニー部分は緊急時の避難や救助を兼ねた多機能なファサードとなる。その表情が、街並みに積極的に参加する新しい病院の顔となることを意識した。

In a typical four-bed room, there is a big disparity in comfort between the window-side bed and hallway-side bed. In our plan, we provided openings on walls along the hallway to let in and diffuse the indirect light coming from the courtyard to the hallway-side beds. For window-side beds, we combined balconies and vertical louvers to provide shade and secure privacy. The balconies are multifunctional facades that also serve as evacuation and rescue routes in case of emergency. The design concept expresses a new look for the hospital, one that actively engages with its surrounding urban landscape.

113

# 日本基督教団 真駒内教会

United Church of Christ in Japan,
Makomanai Church

———

2014

———

配置図 / Site location plan S=1:15000

北外観 / North facade

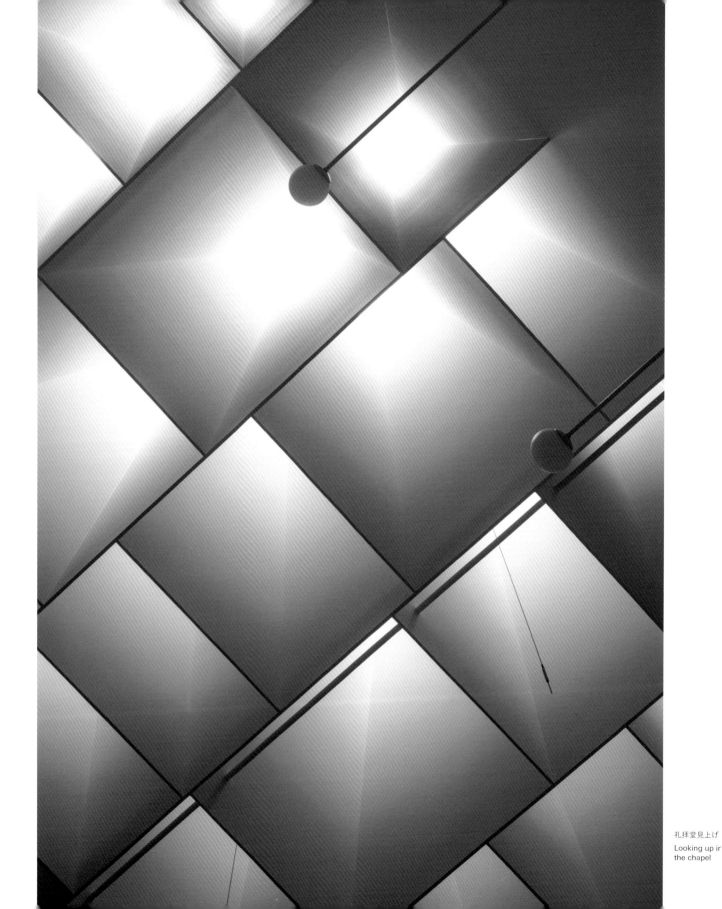

礼拝堂見上げ
Looking up in
the chapel

礼拝堂天井面には深い光井戸を設け、刻々と変わる光で満たすことを試みた。光井戸を構成する小さなトップライトと深いフィンは、夏至の頃の南中時にのみ、直接光線を床に届ける。東西に向けたトップライトは、それぞれ直接光と天空光を取り込み、午前と午後で光線の色の違いが入れ替わる。異なる角度でできたフィンは教会にふさわしい残響をもたらし、また深さがあることで熱の緩衝帯にもなっている。トップライトの勾配は雪を落とすため45度とし、雪を溜める大きな樋が、連続する外観の三角形を形成する。光が、時に強く、時にはかなく、人々を分け隔てなく照らし、礼拝堂を出ると季節ごとの色彩が人々を迎える。

Deep light wells were set on the ceiling of the chapel in an effort to fill it with light that changes moment by moment. The small skylights and deep fins that make up the light wells deliver direct rays to the floor only during the meridian passage of the summer solstice. The skylights facing east and west take in direct and reflected light respectively, with the light rays changing color and switching from the morning into the afternoon. The fins set at various angles produce echoes befitting the church and, with their depth, serve as a thermal buffer zone as well. The slope of the skylight is set at 45 degrees to let the snow slide down the roof. The large gutters that collect the snow form a series of triangles on the facade. The light, sometimes strong and sometimes ephemeral, shines down equally on all the people, and welcomes them with the seasonal colors as they leave the chapel.

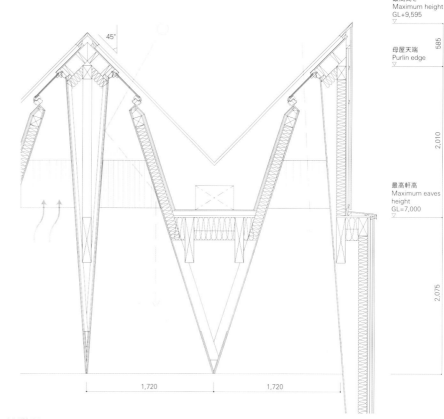

最高高さ
Maximum height
GL+9,595

母屋天端
Purlin edge

最高軒高
Maximum eaves height
GL=7,000

585

2,010

2,075

45°

1,720　1,720

トップライト詳細図 / Detailed drawing of the skylights　S=1:50

1. 礼拝堂
   Chapel
2. ホワイエ
   Foyer
3. 集会室
   Meeting room
4. 牧師館
   Vicarage

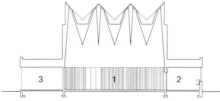
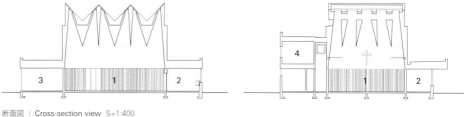

断面図 / Cross-section view　S=1:400

光の移り変わり / Transition of light

ホワイエ / Foyer

礼拝堂は日々使われる教会活動を支える諸室で囲まれている。日曜に行われる礼拝を厳しい寒さから守るためである。各々独自の角度をもつ周囲の建築や境界線と平行させた平面、人々を迎える屋根から続く庇、光井戸をつくるための条件からもたらされるファサードは、この場所の環境とそれに応える合理でかたちづくられたものである。

The chapel is surrounded by rooms that are used daily to support the church's activities. This was designed to protect the Sunday church services from the harsh cold. The floor plan that runs parallel to the boundary lines and surrounding buildings, which have their own respective angles; the eaves that extend from the roof to welcome the people; and the facade that was conceived out of the conditions for creating the light wells—all of these were shaped by the environment of this place and by the rational response to it.

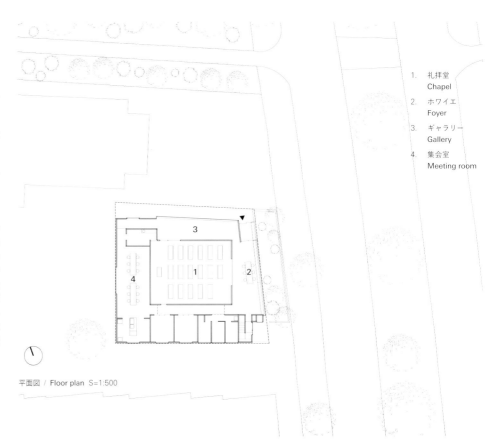

1. 礼拝堂
   Chapel
2. ホワイエ
   Foyer
3. ギャラリー
   Gallery
4. 集会室
   Meeting room

平面図 / Floor plan S=1:500

礼拝堂 / Chapel

西外観 / West facade

東外観 / East facade

北東外観 / Northeast facade

## "亜寒帯のシェルター"その先へ

小澤丈夫

アトリエブンク（以下BNK）による作品集『Atelier BNK 2000-2014』と、新作品集『Atelier BNK 2014-2022』のゲラが手元にある。『2000-2014』は、加藤誠の論文「亜寒帯のシェルター」と15作品による、21世紀の積雪寒冷地の建築のあり方を見据えたBNKのマニフェストであった。筆者が寄せた拙稿では、作品発表時に個人名を出さず、アトリエを設計活動のインフラとみなし、メンバーがひとつの傘のもとで、建築デザインを追求する姿をラボラトリーに見立てた。1970年の創設以来、BNKは多様なメンバーの個性を併存させ、多くの建築作品を生み出してきたが、加藤が表明した探究の方向性によって、そこに留まらない発展性、慎重でややストイックな態度、ロジック、作品性が現れていると思われたからである。それから8年、『Atelier BNK 2014-2022』を俯瞰し、新たな展開が見られるように感じた。

### ビルディングタイプの多様化・視野の広がりと深み

まず、BNKが長年探究してきた積雪寒冷地における建築技術とデザイン手法が、一定の居住性と建物の耐久性を担保できる段階に達したことに加え、ビルディングタイプが多様になり、視野の広がりと深みが見られるようになった点があげられよう。『2014-2022』には、これまでになかった、役場、地区再開発、テクノロジーファーム、病院、教会などがある。「芽室町役場」(2021)では、日高山脈を望む大地に刻まれたグリッド状の都市空間に役場を位置づけ、遠景、中景、近景との関係の中に、各階で異なる空間の広がりをもたせている。

制震ダンパーを外周部に置くことによって実現した開放的な内部空間は、外部とつながりながらも守られ、取り込まれた眺望と自然光、仕上げの素材感によって、おおらかで快適な居住性を獲得している。「滝川市栄町3-3地区再開発事業」(2018)は、建物ボリューム、溜まりとなる屋外空間、オープンな動線がシンプルに構成され、景観的、空間的に全体が慎ましくすっきりと纏められている。「幌東病院」(2017)は、必要な高い機能性を担保しつつ、水平に伸びる庇、縦ルーバー、縦長の窓をもつ4層の全体ボリュームの中に、患者と医療スタッフのためのホスピタリティ溢れる居場所が、随所に心地よいスケールでつくられている。「真駒内教会」(2014)は、BNKがこれまで実践してきた入子状の空間構成をもち、中央の礼拝堂にトップライトを通して降り注ぐ直接光と反射光が、天候や時間によって刻々と変化し空間を彩る様子が印象的である。探究を繰り返してきた高所からの採光がもたらす効果が、抽象度の高い礼拝堂の空間において遺憾なく発揮されている。

### 発展する"亜寒帯のシェルター"

材料面、構造面でも新たな展開が見られる。これまでは、コンクリート、鉄骨、板金、ガラス等の無機的な材料を外装に用い、外観を複数の異なる形態のボリュームの組み合わせとして見せる傾向があった。水平に広がる低層の全体ボリューム、冬季に雪を貯える厚い庇、高く隆起する屋根形状などには、積雪寒冷地において普遍化しうる建築デザインをシンプルに定義したいという明快な意志があった。ここに、新しく木材やレンガなどの外装材、小さなスケールをもつ開口部等が付加され、これまでより複合的な表情が見られるようになった。構造形式では、これまではRC、鉄骨、大断面集成材によるロングスパンが空間を特徴づけていたが、道内の一般流通木材・集成材を積極的に用いる新たなテーマのもと、木造架構がもつ小さなスケール感が併存するようになった。外周部のRC造と内部の木造を混構造にした「津別町役場」(2022)の独立柱と頬杖、吹き抜けに露出する水平材、RC造のホールを木造で囲んだ「鷹栖地区

住民センター」(2019)の読書室に現れるトラス架構などが注目される。このように、建物に求められる用途や機能に応じ、材料や構造形式を適材適所に使い分け複合化することによって、2014年に宣言された"亜寒帯のシェルター"が、発展している姿をここに捉えることができよう。

### 感覚に訴えかける建築へ

写真のフレーミングやレイアウトの変化によって、多様なシーンを表現している点にも注目したい。近年のBNKは、各プロジェクトにおける参画のしかたや設計与条件への関わり方を発展的に強化しているようだ。写真表現の変化には、建築家の職能の枠組みを広げ、空間デザインをより総合化しようとする意識を見ることができるように思われる。ここで、やや唐突な言及かもしれないが、かつてペーター・ツムトアが表明した概念"Atmosphaeren"（邦訳：空気感、雰囲気）が思い出された。その講義録の編者は、「ペーター・ツムトアの建築とそれをとりまく環境のあいだには相互作用がある。与えあい、受け取り合う。交換がある。たがいが豊かになる。」と述べている。ツムトア自身は、人間が生き延びるために必要とする情緒的な感覚に訴える"Atmosphaeren"を考えるとき、特にそこを訪れる人の第一印象こそが大切だと言う。そうだとするならば、BNKが築きあげてきた積雪寒冷地における建築技術とデザイン手法が一定のレベルに達した今、"亜寒帯のシェルター"というマニフェストを超え、生み出される建築が、どのように訪れる人の感覚に訴えかけ、総合的かつ有機的になり得えているかを主題として評価すべき時期にきているのかもしれない。

# Beyond "Shelters in the Subarctic"

Takeo OZAWA

I have with me the "Atelier BNK 2000–2014" collection of works as well as the book galley of the new collection, "Atelier BNK 2014–2022," created by Atelier BNK (hereafter "BNK"). "2000–2014" was BNK's manifesto, which envisions the ideal architecture in cold, snowy regions for the 21st century, and contains Makoto Kato's essay "Shelters in the Subarctic" and 15 other works. In the manuscript I submitted, individual names were not mentioned when presenting works; instead, the atelier was regarded as the infrastructure of all design undertakings and likened to a laboratory with team members pursuing architectural design under one umbrella. Since its founding in 1970, BNK has produced numerous architectural works through coexistence between its diverse members' distinct personalities. This can be attributed to the unfettered possibilities, deliberate and slightly stoic approach, logic, and artistry that emerges, through the exploratory direction expressed by Kato. Eight years have passed since then, and looking at the overall picture of "Atelier BNK 2014–2022," I sense the unfolding of new developments.

## Diversifying types of buildings, and a broader and deeper scope

First of all, BNK's explorations over the years on building technologies and architectural design techniques for cold, snowy regions have reached a stage where a level of livability and building durability can be ensured. Moreover, the types of buildings have diversified. This has led to a broader and deeper scope. The "2014–2022" collection includes their first-ever town hall, district redevelopment, technology farm, hospital, church, and many others. In Memuro Town Hall (2021), which is located on a grid-like urban space carved out of a broad land overlooking the Hidaka Mountains, each floor offers a different sequence of space relative to the view, from the distant panorama to the middle distance and the foreground. The open interior space—achieved by placing seismic control dampers on the building periphery—is protected while being connected with the outside. The captured view, natural light, and texture of finishings provide relaxation and comfort. In Takikawa City Sakae-Machi 3-3 District Redevelopment Project (2018), the building volume, outdoor space for gatherings, and open movement routes are simple in composition, with the overall landscape and space arranged in a clean and modest style. Koto Hospital (2017) was designed for an intimate scale at every location, and is a place filled with hospitality for patients and medical staff within an overall volume of four stories, featuring horizontal extended eaves, vertical louvers, and vertically long windows while also fulfilling requirements for high performance. Makomanai Church (2014) has a nested spatial composition, which has been carried out by BNK over the years. The direct and reflected light falling through the skylights and into the central chapel changes moment by moment according to the time and weather, providing a striking display of colors in the space. The effects of aerial natural light, which they have repeatedly explored, is perfectly demonstrated in the highly abstract space of the chapel.

## Evolving "Shelters in the Subarctic"

New developments can be seen in terms of materials and structures as well. Previously, inorganic materials such as concrete, steel frames, sheet metal, and glass have been used for exteriors. Thus, exteriors featured facades made up of a combination of volumes in several different forms. Elements such as the overall volume of low buildings that spread out horizontally, thick eaves that accumulate snow in winter, and the shape of roofs thrusting upward showed a clear desire to define architectural designs in simple terms that can be universalized for cold, snowy regions. Now, new cladding materials such as wood and brick, small-scale apertures, and so on have been added to produce more complex expressions. For structural forms, spaces which have previously been characterized by long spans made of reinforced concrete, steel frames, or large laminated timber, now also coexist with wooden frames that provide a sense of the small-scale, under a new design theme of actively using commercial wood and laminated timber within Hokkaido. Noted examples of these are the isolated columns, braces, and exposed horizontal members in the atrium of Tsubetsu Town Hall (2022), a mixed structure with a reinforced concrete peripheral structure and a wooden internal structure, and the truss frames visible in the reading room of Takasu District Residents Center (2019), a reinforced concrete hall surrounded by a wooden structure. In this way, the "Shelters in the Subarctic" professed in 2014 can be seen here in an evolved form, through the judicious use, placement, and combination of materials and structural forms, according to the purpose and functions required of the building.

Atelier BNK | 2000–2014

## Toward architecture that appeals to the senses

I would also like to point out that a variety of scenes are portrayed through the changes in the framing and layout of the photographs. In recent years, BNK seems to be developing and enhancing ways to get involved in each project and engage with design requirements. This change in photographic expression may be seen as an intent to broaden the framework of the architect's profession and to make spatial design more comprehensive. This may be a bit out of the blue, but it reminds me of the concept of "Atmosphären" ("Atmospheres" in English), which was once expressed by Peter Zumthor. The editor of the lecture transcript wrote, "There is an exchange, a give-and-take, between Peter Zumthor's buildings and their surroundings. An attentiveness. An enrichment." Zumthor himself says that when thinking about "Atmosphären" that are perceived through our emotional sensibilities—which we humans need for survival—first impressions of visitors are especially important. If so, now that the building technologies and architectural design techniques for cold, snowy regions that BNK has built up over the years have reached a certain level, perhaps it is time to go beyond the "Shelters in the Subarctic" manifesto and evaluate how the architecture produced can appeal to visitors' senses, and become integral and organic.

小澤丈夫（おざわ たけお）
建築家／北海道大学大学院教授

1961年兵庫県生まれ。東京工業大学大学院修士課程修了、1996年ベルラーへ建築研究所アムステルダム修了、1994年ヘルマン・ヘルツベルハー建築設計事務所、1997年 TEO architects 設立（共同主宰小澤エリ子、2013年 office teo に改称）。2005年 北海道大学大学院准教授、2016年同教授。主な研究分野にスイスドイツ語圏における空間計画体系と空間デザイン手法に関する研究、戦後北海道の近代建築の発展と建築家に関する研究、代表作：丘のまち交流館"bi.yell"、北海道大学医学部百年記念館、著書に『現代板金建築 THE BANKIN』『Atsuta/research and design, re-vision of Hokkaido』など。

**Takeo OZAWA**
Architect, Professor at Hokkaido University Faculty of Engineering

Born in Hyogo Prefecture in 1961. After graduating with a master's degree at the Graduate School of the Tokyo Institute of Technology, he finished his studies at the Berlage Institute, Amsterdam in 1996. He joined Architectuurstudio Herman Hertzberger in 1994, and then founded TEO architects in 1997 (co-presided with Eriko Ozawa), which was renamed office teo in 2013. In 2005, he became an Associate Professor, then a Professor in 2016 at the Hokkaido University Faculty of Engineering. His main research fields are on spatial planning systems and spatial design methods in the Swiss German region, and on architects and modern architectural development in postwar Hokkaido. His major works include bi.yell, a hillside town community center; and Hokkaido University School of Medicine Centennial Hall. His publications include "Contemporary Japanese Bankin (Sheet Metal) Architecture THE BANKIN" and "Atsuta/research and design, re-vision of Hokkaido."

## 作品概要
### List of Project

**芽室町役場**
竣工年：2021

北海道河西郡芽室町

構造：S＋RC　地下1階・地上3階
延床面積：4,734㎡

建築：アトリエブンク・創造設計舎　設計JV
構造：金箱構造設計事務所
設備：アトリエブンク＋総合設備計画
外構：プラッツ
音響：永田音響設計
環境アドヴァイザー：北方建築総合研究所
サイン：KD

施工（建築）：宮坂・北土・鍵谷　特定JV

―――――――

**ニセコ町役場**
竣工年：2021

北海道虻田郡ニセコ町

構造：RC　地下1階・地上3階
延床面積：3,374㎡

構造：金箱構造設計事務所
設備：アトリエブンク＋総合設備計画
外構：キタバ・ランドスケープ
音響：永田音響設計
環境アドヴァイザー：北方建築総合研究所
サイン：KD

施工（建築）：泰進・浦野・石塚　特定JV

―――――――

**津別町役場**
竣工年：2022

北海道網走郡津別町

構造：W＋RC　地上2階
延床面積：3,260㎡

構造：金箱構造設計事務所
設備：アトリエブンク＋総合設備計画
環境アドヴァイザー：北方建築総合研究所

施工（建築）：津別・三共後藤・五十嵐　特定JV

―――――――

**夕張市拠点複合施設 りすた**
竣工年：2019

北海道夕張市

構造：S　地上1階
延床面積：1,700㎡

基本構想：北海道大学都市地域デザイン学研究室
構造：山脇克彦建築構造設計
設備：アトリエブンク＋総合設備計画
外構（基本設計）：キタバ・ランドスケープ

施工（建築）：ピーエス三菱・坂本建設工業　特定JV

日本建築学会作品選集 2021-2022
JIA建築年鑑 2021-2022

―――――――

**鷹栖地区住民センター**
竣工年：2019

北海道上川郡鷹栖町

構造：RC＋W　地上1階
延床面積：2,060㎡

構造：山脇克彦建築構造設計
設備：アトリエブンク＋総合設備計画
外構：プラッツ
音響：永田音響設計
環境アドヴァイザー：北方建築総合研究所

施工（建築）：高・畠山・菅原　特定JV

日本建築学会作品選集 2021-2022
JIA建築年鑑 2021-2022
新建築 201905
新・建築設計資料 01

―――――――

**上士幌町生涯学習センター わっか**
竣工年：2017

北海道河東郡上士幌町

構造：W＋RC　地上2階
延床面積：4,122㎡（うち既存部　1,791㎡）

基本計画：北海道大学建築計画学研究室
構造：金箱構造設計事務所
設備：アトリエブンク＋アルス・ゼータ
外構：プラッツ

施工（建築）：萩原・川田・橘内・米倉　経常JV
　　（改修）：ネクサス・森岡建設　経常JV

JIA建築年鑑 2019-2020

**黒松内町庁舎耐震改修・コミュニティ防災センター**
竣工年：2015

北海道寿都郡黒松内町

構造：既存部　RC＋W（roof）、増築部　RC　地上2階
延床面積：1,680㎡（うち既存部　671㎡）

構造：金箱構造設計事務所
設備：アトリエブンク＋総合設備計画

施工（建築）：田中組・スガワラ・久光工業　特定JV

―――――――

**北海道札幌視覚支援学校**
竣工年：2015

北海道札幌市

構造：RC＋S　地上3階
延床面積：12,634㎡

構造：金箱構造設計事務所
設備：アトリエブンク＋環境設備計画
外構（基本設計）：アトリエブンク＋プラッツ

施工（建築）：校舎1工区　岩倉・石山　特定JV
　　　　　　　校舎2工区　岩田地崎・鈴木東建　特定JV
　　　　　　　校舎3工区　伊藤組土建
　　　　　　　寄宿舎1工区・理療研修センター　岩倉建設
　　　　　　　寄宿舎2工区　丸竹竹田組
　　　　　　　寄宿舎3工区・体育館　中山組
　　　　　　　専攻科棟　丸彦渡辺・泰進　経常JV
　　　　　　　プール　武ダ技建創

―――――――

**利尻小学校・鬼脇中学校**
竣工年：2018

北海道利尻郡利尻富士町

構造：RC、SRC　地上2階
延床面積：4,470㎡

構造：札幌構造設計事務所
設備：アトリエブンク＋総合設備計画
外構：アトリエブンク＋GTアドヴァンス

施工（建築）：石塚・中田・雨森・山本　経常JV

―――――――

**名寄南小学校**
竣工年：2016

北海道名寄市

構造：RC+SRC+S　地上3階
延床面積：8,338㎡

構造：札幌構造設計事務所
設備：アトリエブンク＋総合設備計画
外構：アトリエブンク＋GTアドヴァンス

施工（建築）：1工区　新井・大野組・坂下　特定JV
　　　　　　　2工区　廣野・大野土建・橋本川島・
　　　　　　　　　　　高橋組　特定JV

---

**開西中学校**
竣工年：2015

北海道滝川市

構造：RC+S　地上3階
延床面積：5,624㎡（うち既存部　2,924㎡）

建築：ブンク・アキバ　特定JV
構造：金箱構造設計事務所
設備：アトリエブンク＋総合設備計画
外構：アトリエブンク＋GTアドヴァンス

施工（建築）：中山・泰進　経常JV

---

**厚沢部町認定こども園 はぜる**
竣工年：2018

北海道檜山郡厚沢部町

構造：W　地上1階
延床面積：1,480㎡

構造：海老名構造研究室
設備：アトリエブンク＋アルス・ゼータ
外構：アトリエブンク＋GTアドヴァンス

施工（建築）：高橋・能登谷・厚峰　経常JV

---

**北星学園大学キャンパスリノベーション**
竣工年：2015

北海道札幌市

構造：S　新C館＋A館 地上7階・地下1階、
　　　　　　　　　　　センター棟 地上2階
延床面積：新C館＋A館　21,121㎡（うち既存部13,659㎡）
　　　　　　センター棟　1,368㎡（改修）
構造：金箱構造設計事務所
設備：アトリエブンク＋アルス・ゼータ
外構：ブラッツ
音響：永田音響設計

施工：一期　新C館新築＋A館改修　清水建設北海道支店
　　　二期　センター棟改修＋カバードウォーク
　　　　　　岩田地崎建設
　　　三期　守衛所＋外構　清水建設北海道支店

---

**滝川市栄町3-3地区再開発事業**
竣工年：2018

北海道滝川市

医療介護棟
構造：RC　地上3階・地下1階
延床面積：5,695㎡
金融機関棟
構造：S　地上6階
延床面積：3,749㎡

基本構想：コンパクトシティ
構造：札幌構造設計事務所
設備：アトリエブンク＋総合設備計画
外構：アトリエブンク＋GTアドヴァンス

施工：医療介護棟　泰進建設
　　　金融機関棟　中山・田端本堂・笹木　特定JV

---

**テクノロジーファーム 西の里**
竣工年：2018

北海道北広島市

構造：S　地上2階
延床面積：3,234㎡

構造：札幌構造設計事務所
設備：アトリエブンク＋アド・エンジニアリング
外構：アトリエブンク＋GTアドヴァンス

施工：松村組

---

**ウポポイ　体験交流ホール**
竣工年：2019

北海道白老郡白老町

構造：S　地上2階
延床面積：1,666㎡

企画・監修：国土交通省北海道開発局
建築・設備：アトリエブンク・総合設備計画　JV
構造：山脇克彦建築構造設計
音響：永田音響設計

施工（建築）：伊藤組土建

新建築202009

---

**幌東病院**
竣工年：2017

北海道札幌市

構造：RC+S　地下1階・地上4階
延床面積：9,822㎡

構造：金箱構造設計事務所
設備：アトリエブンク＋総合設備計画
外構：ブラッツ
家具：伊藤千織＋匠工芸

施工：伊藤組土建

日本建築学会作品選集2019
JIA建築年鑑2019
新建築201712
建築ジャーナル201810

---

**日本基督教団 真駒内教会**
竣工年：2014

北海道札幌市

構造：W　地上2階
延床面積：384㎡

構造：都市構造研究所
設備：アトリエブンク＋アルス・ゼータ
音響：永田音響設計

施工：クワザワ工業

ディテール220号
日本建築学会作品選集2018
JIA建築年鑑2017

## 主な受賞歴　[2014-2022]
Prize

2021
北海道赤レンガ建築奨励賞（ニセコ町役場）

2020
北海道赤レンガ建築賞（夕張市拠点複合施設 りすた）

2020
公共建築協会 公共建築賞優秀賞（北海道札幌視覚支援学校）

2020
公共建築協会 公共建築賞優秀賞（東川小学校・東川町地域交流センター）

2019
北海道赤レンガ建築奨励賞（東川町複合交流施設せんとぴゅあ）

2019
日本建築家協会 JIA25年賞（二風谷アイヌ文化博物館）

2018
北海道赤レンガ建築賞（上士幌町生涯学習センター わっか）

2018
日本建築学会作品選奨（日本基督教団 真駒内教会）

2018
公共建築協会 公共建築賞優秀賞（豊富定住支援センター）

2016
北海道建築奨励賞（日本基督教団 真駒内教会）

2016
公共建築協会 公共建築賞優秀賞（函館市縄文文化交流センター）

2015
北海道赤レンガ建築奨励賞（東川小学校・東川町地域交流センター）

2014
北海道赤レンガ建築奨励賞（豊富定住支援センター）

2021
Hokkaido Red Brick Architecture Award (Niseko Town Hall)

2020
Hokkaido Red Brick Architecture Award (Yubari City Community Base Complex RESTA)

2020
Public Building Award Excellence Prize (Hokkaido Sapporo Special Needs School for the Visually Impaired)

2020
Public Building Award Excellence Prize (Higashikawa Elementary School and Higashikawa Community Center)

2019
Hokkaido Red Brick Architecture Award (Higashikawa Cultural Exchange Center)

2019
JIA Twenty-five Year Award (Nibutani Ainu Culture Museum)

2018
Hokkaido Red Brick Architecture Award (Kamishihoro Lifelong Learning Center Wakka)

2018
Annual Architectural Design Commendation of the Architectural Institute of Japan (United Church of Christ in Japan, Makomanai Church)

2018
Public Building Award Excellence Prize (Toyotomi Community Center)

2016
Hokkaido Architecture Award (United Church of Christ in Japan, Makomanai Church)

2016
Public Building Award Excellence Prize (Hakodate Jomon Culture Center)

2015
Hokkaido Red Brick Architecture Award (Higashikawa Elementary School and Higashikawa Community Center)

2014
Hokkaido Red Brick Architecture Award (Toyotomi Community Center)

## 会社概要
## Company Profile

1970年に秋山孝、後藤達也、濱田暁生によって札幌で創設以来、北海道を中心に建築設計の活動を続けてきた。事務所開設当初は住宅やインテリアの仕事が中心であったが、1980年代以降徐々に公共的な建築を手がける機会を増やし現在に至る。手がけた作品は様々な評価を与えられてきた。日本建築学会作品選奨4作品、日本建築学会作品選集23作品、公共建築賞優秀賞11作品、JIA環境建築賞などがあり、また地域の賞としては北海道建築賞／奨励賞を10作品、北海道赤レンガ建築賞／奨励賞を9作品受賞している。2013年、2022年に個展を開催し、また2014年には作品集『Atelier BNK 2000-2014』(建築画報社) を出版した。

Based in Hokkaido, Atelier BNK has been actively working in architectural design since Takashi Akiyama, Tatsuya Goto, and Akio Hamada founded the studio in Sapporo in 1970. Initially, the design studio mainly worked on residential houses and interiors, although opportunities to work on public buildings gradually increased from the 1980s until the present day. The works of BNK has been praised from various quarters. Four of its works have received the AIJ Annual Architectural Design Commendation, 23 works have appeared in the Selected Architectural Designs of AIJ, 11 have won the Public Building Award Excellence Prize, and one has won the JIA Sustainable Architecture Award, among other awards. For regional prizes, 10 works received the Hokkaido Architecture Award/Encouragement Award, while nine other works received the Hokkaido Red Brick Architecture Award/Encouragement Award. BNK has also held exhibitions in 2013 and 2022, as well as published a collection of works called "Atelier BNK 2000–2014" (published by Kenchiku Gahou Inc.) in 2014.

www.atelier-bnk.co.jp

## アトリエブンク スタッフ
Atelier BNK Staff

Staff August, 2022

| | |
|---|---|
| Akihiro Tanikawa | 谷川　明弘 |
| Akira Hasegawa | 長谷川　明 |
| Atsuki Kojima | 小島　厚樹 |
| Ayako Nagashima | 長島　綾子 |
| Fumihiro Miyamoto | 宮本　史大 |
| Hideki Suganuma | 菅沼　秀樹 |
| Hiroaki Fuzawa | 麩澤　宏明 |
| Hiroshi Misu | 三栖　博 |
| Ikuya Hiraiwa | 平岩　郁也 |
| Kana Asato | 安里　佳菜 |
| Kazuhiko Osawa | 大澤　一彦 |
| Keita Toda | 戸田　啓太 |
| Kensho Kawasari | 川去　健翔 |
| Kumiko Uchida | 内田　久美子 |
| Makoto Kato | 加藤　誠 |
| Masato Fukuyama | 福山　将斗 |
| Masaya Yoshida | 吉田　正哉 |
| Misato Kitagawa | 北川　美怜 |
| Mitsutoshi Ikehata | 池畠　光俊 |
| Miyuki Inagaki | 稲垣　美幸 |
| Nana Ikemura | 池村　菜々 |
| Nicole Checo | チェコ　ニコル |
| Norio Kikuchi | 菊池　規雄 |
| Ryoko Yamamoto | 山本　亮子 |
| Sadanori Otsuji | 尾辻　自然 |
| Shingo Hojoh | 北條　真伍 |
| Shinji Hatakeyama | 畠山　進次 |
| Shoma Yamauchi | 山内　翔馬 |
| Taichi Miura | 三浦　太一 |
| Takashi Akiyama | 秋山　孝 |
| Takeshi Murakuni | 村國　健 |
| Tatsuya Goto | 後藤　達也 |
| Yoshihiro Kimura | 木村　良博 |
| Yukihiro Takahashi | 高橋　幸宏 |
| Yurika Aoto | 青砥　由里香 |

[2014–2022 Former staff]

| | |
|---|---|
| Atsushi Wada | 和田　敦 |
| Chika Yamada | 山田　知加 |
| Harumi Narigasawa | 成ヶ澤　はるみ |
| Hiroki Kitahama | 北濱　広樹 |
| Kenichi Yamazaki | 山﨑　謙一 |
| Kenta Takeuchi | 竹内　健太 |
| Konomi Kato | 加藤　このみ |
| Masaaki Izumi | 泉　正明 |
| Masahiro Amasaki | 天崎　正博 |
| Masanori Nakaoka | 中岡　正憲 |
| Megumi Takeshita | 竹下　恵 |
| Osamu Noro | 野呂　修 |
| Saori Date | 伊達　紗央里 |
| Shunsuke Shibata | 柴田　俊介 |
| Takuya Oyama | 尾山　拓也 |
| Tomo Maruyama | 丸山　智 |
| Tota Sugawara | 菅原　統太 |
| Yoshiyuki Uramoto | 浦本　義幸 |
| Yu Taira | 平　裕 |
| Yui Abo | 阿保　結生 |
| Yutaro Tsuji | 辻　勇太朗 |
| Toshimi Takemura | 竹村　壽美 |